MY REMINISCENCES OF THE G.A.R.

Richard O. Partington

HERITAGE BOOKS
2008

HERITAGE BOOKS
AN IMPRINT OF HERITAGE BOOKS, INC.

Books, CDs, and more—Worldwide

For our listing of thousands of titles see our website at
www.HeritageBooks.com

Published 2008 by
HERITAGE BOOKS, INC.
Publishing Division
100 Railroad Ave. #104
Westminster, Maryland 21157

Copyright © 2004 Richard O. Partington

All rights reserved. No part of this book may be reproduced or transmitted in any form or by any means, electronic or mechanical, including photocopying, recording or by any information storage and retrieval system without written permission from the author, except for the inclusion of brief quotations in a review.

International Standard Book Number: 978-0-7884-2502-8

Dedicated to my daughter S. Lynn Partington without whose hard work in organizing, typing, and improving my poor pictures this manuscript would be impossible.

TABLE OF CONTENTS

Introduction   vii

Chapter

I.   My Reminiscences of the G.A.R.   1

II.   Gettysburg, The 75th Reunion - 1938   39

III.   Diary Kept by William H. H. Ogden, Sr. During the Last Years of His Enlistment, 1862-1864   79

Introduction

From earliest boyhood I was interested in the Civil War. I think a contributing factor in this interest was early association with members of the Grand Army of the Republic. My great grandfather had been active in this organization, and, although he died before my birth, my grandfather, his son, had contributed to my interest by telling me stories about his father and exposing me on various occasions to members of the Grand Army of the Republic.

The men I write about I knew personally and recorded their stories from questions and listening and taking notes at newspaper interviews. There were others that I knew, but regret that I knew little about them.

I have been a member of the Sons of Union Veterans of the Civil War, a congressionally chartered organization of descendents of union veterans and the legal heir of the G.A.R., for over 65 years having served in many capacities in that organization. In 1987-88, I served as Commander-in-Chief of that organization. During this time, it was my privilege to meet many interesting persons including Bruce Catton, noted historian of the Civil War. It was my privilege also to know and to serve on many occasions with Ulysses S. Grant III, Major General, U.S.A. Ret., a past commander-in-chief of the Sons and of Mollus.

I once asked the General if he remembered his grandfather. He said he certainly did, and, although he was only four when he died, he remembered his grandfather taking him piggy-back around the rooms showing his various trophies and explaining what they were for and from whence they came. He also spoke of visiting Mt. McGregor, where his grandfather died, and members of the G.A.R. standing guard to protect him from the curious, and afterward riding in a carriage with his mother in the funeral procession.

The Grand Army of the Republic was the granddaddy of all veteran organizations, but, unlike later veteran organizations, was not opened to veterans of succeeding wars. Here is an explanation of the Grand Army of the Republic printed in a program for the 1939 Encampment held in Pittsburgh, PA.

Grand Army of the Republic heritage

"The Grand Army of the Republic is a unique organization. No child can be born into it. No proclamation of President, edict of King or Czar, can command admission. No university or institution of learning can issue a diploma authorizing its holder to entrance. No act of Parliament or Congress secures recognition. The wealth of a Vanderbilt cannot purchase the position. Its doors open only on the presentation of the bit of parchment, worn, torn, and begrimed as it may be, which certifies to an honorable discharge from the armies or navies of the Nation during the war against the rebellion, and unlike any other organization, no new blood can come in. There are no growing ranks from which recruits can be drawn into the Grand Army of the Republic. With the consummation of peace through victory its ranks were closed forever; its lines are steadily growing thinner, and the ceaseless tramp of its columns is with ever-lessening tread. The gaps in the picket lines grow wider every day. Details are made for the reserve summoned into the shadowy regions until by and by only a solitary sentinel will stand guard, waiting until the bugle call from beyond shall muster out the last comrade of the Grand Army of the Republic."

Anonymous

When I attended the 75th Reunion of the Blue and Gray in Gettysburg in 1938, I had a little diary and a small camera. As I went around the encampment, I tried to interview some of the veterans and get their signatures. I also took pictures of some of them.

At the time I was only a teenager and photography was not my forte which is true even to this day. Some of the pictures of the veterans were not of the best quality and have aged since then. They have been reproduced on the following pages along with the notes from that diary.

Chapter I
My Reminiscences of the G.A.R.

The Union Veterans were scarcely out of uniform before they began to form various veteran groups in order to influence the voting in the 1866 election. Even though soon after the election many of these groups disbanded, there remained the desire for continuous comradeship which was formed during the war. This was the motivation which lead to the organization of many early G.A.R. posts.

The first G.A.R. post was organized at Decatur, Illinois, in April 1866 by Major Benjamin F. Stephenson who had been a surgeon with the Illinois Infantry. Shortly afterwards he chartered Post No. 2 at Springfield, Illinois. These two posts were the foundation upon which the national organization was organized.

The first encampment of the GAR was held in Indianapolis in 1866. General S. A. Hurlbut was elected Commander-in-Chief. He was a Major General during the Civil War, and was later elected as a member of Congress from Illinois.

Perhaps the best known Commander-in-Chief was General John A. Logan from Illinois who was the second Commander-in-Chief. He was a Democratic member of Congress when the War began and rose rapidly to the rank of Major General. He was the only Commander-in-Chief to serve three terms. After the War, he was elected U.S. Senator from that State, and was the Republican nominee for Vice-president in 1884. Although it may be difficult to ascribe to any one individual the honor of originating the beautiful custom of decorating the graves of the heroic dead who were willing to sacrifice their lives for their country, it was General Logan who issued General Order Number 11 designating a certain day, May 30th, as Memorial Day.

After the Revolutionary War as well as the war of 1812 and the Mexican War, the veterans would have various reunions and observe the anniversaries of various battles, but it remained for the veterans of the Civil War to form a Veteran's Organization. This Veteran's Organization was called the Grand Army of the Republic. Its purpose was to work for the welfare of the veterans of that war.

It must be remembered that at the end of the war, there was no provision to furnish the discharged Union Soldier with any of his needs. He had no hospitalization, no allowance for education or training or vocational rehabilitation. They were granted no loans for the purchase or reconstruction of houses, no temporary housing, no allowance for unemployment, no national service life insurance, no government loans of money, no preference in the Civil Service for either himself or his wife, no preference in the sale of surplus war material, no allowance for widows or dependent children. A friend of mine, a past Commander-in-Chief of the Sons of Union Veterans of the Civil War, Walter C. Mabie, who is now deceased, carried a pile of membership cards at least an inch thick indicating his membership in various fraternal and charitable organizations. When I asked why so many organizations, he told me this story. His father returned from the Civil War broken in health, and died shortly afterwards leaving his wife a widow with several dependent children. They had no money or other means of support. His comrades from the Grand Army of the Republic took up a collection and bought his mother a small store and stocked it with candy and other small items so that she could make a small living to support herself and the children. He never forgot this, and this is why he belonged to so many fraternal and charitable organizations.

The Grand Army was vigorous in advocating pensions for needy veterans, but it was also generous with its own funds on behalf of crippled and needy veterans. As early as 1873, when it was operating on a shoestring, $48,000 was given to charity by various posts. There wasn't any government allowance in those days to provide for a needy veteran or his family after he was gone.

It is true that public lands were opened to the returning veteran. He could claim 160 acres of the public land, and this they did by the thousands. They went to the new states of Kansas, Nebraska, Colorado, the Dakotas, and to the far Pacific states. It wasn't until many years after the war, through the efforts of the Grand Army of the Republic, that pensions were granted at first to disabled veterans and finally to their widows and children. After the war they rehabilitated themselves, and in so doing, they rehabilitated the nation.

In the early history of the Grand Army of the Republic, many of its leaders and active members were generals. In later years, the commanders-in-chief were elected from the rank and file. They were younger men and were not available to serve in the early years of the organization.

The largest attendance of any encampment of the Grand Army of the Republic was at Columbus, Ohio in September 1888. Here is a partial description of that Encampment. "The day after the parade, there were headlines in the Columbus papers as follows: 'Without a parallel, the Grand Review at Washington is said not to surpass that of yesterday - 70,000 men salute the Commander-in-Chief! Over 200,000 strangers present, at a low estimate!'" Among the distinguished men on the reviewing stand were General William T. Sherman, Ex-President Rutherford B. Hayes and Mrs. Hayes, General A. P. Hovey of Indiana, Mrs. General John A. Logan and son, General Fred D. Grant and Mrs. Grant, General Russell A. Alger of Michigan, Governor Warren Miller of New York, Senator Allen G. Thurman, and many others.

Columbus was then a city of 80,000 and to accommodate the crowd was quite a feat. Mrs. Foraker, wife of Ohio's governor said that she had major generals sleeping on cots in all parts of her home. The Commander-in-Chief of the G.A.R. at that time was William Warner of Missouri, afterwards a U.S. Senator.

In those days, the railroads contributed their share to the large attendance at National Encampments. A rate of one cent a mile with a sixty day return limit, was granted to all members of the Allied Organizations. This was done on the certificate plan, and required a validation at the Encampment city before starting the return trip. Thus the blue uniform and the black slouch hat of the veterans were conspicuous in the encampment city for two months after the close of the Encampment. The sixty day return limit was used to visit relatives and friends. (See Michael G Heintz - Banner, S.U.V.C.W., 1950)

My association with the Grand Army of the Republic came at a much later date. I attended my first Grand Army Encampment in 1939, when only a few thousand veterans were still living. The veterans I knew were mostly from Pennsylvania particularly from Philadelphia.

The first Post in Pennsylvania, according to information received from the National Program of the 33rd National Encampment held in Philadelphia in 1899, was Post #1 of Philadelphia, and was chartered by Major B.F. Stephenson as Commander-in-Chief, October 16, 1866. Again referring to the National Program, Post #2 was organized October 29, 1866 again in Philadelphia. Although Post #1 became known as the General George G Meade Post, Post #2 never adopted any name but was known by its number only. Post #3 was the General Alexander Hays Post and was organized in Pittsburgh November 3, 1866. The Department of Pennsylvania, G.A.R. was organized in Philadelphia January 16, 1867 at 5th and Chestnut Streets in the Old City Hall, located next to Independence Hall. In 1877, General U. S. Grant, ex-president of the United States was mustered into Meade Post in Independence Hall where he was greeted by many veterans.

The Grand Army of the Republic was an important part of my boyhood and youth. It is my memory of the G.A.R. especially as it relates to Memorial Day and some of the veterans I knew personally that I want to share with you. These memories have been reinforced by personal notes as well as old newspaper articles. My earliest recollection of the Grand Army of the Republic goes back to my grammar school days when veterans of the Civil War although few in number and bent with age would visit the schools prior to Memorial Day. They would be accompanied by younger veterans of the Spanish American War and World War I. Here were men who had answered Lincoln's call for volunteers and who had fought under McClellan at Antietam, with Meade at Gettysburg, who had marched with Sherman to the sea, and who had been with Grant at Appomatox - names which I had read in my history book. Was it any wonder that as a boy, I looked to these aged heroes with awe and fascination.

There was a Grand Army man who lived in our neighborhood, Comrade J. W. Meckert, 5500 Willows Avenue and a member of Captain Phillip R. Schuyler Post 51, who would walk to the neighborhood shopping avenue. Occasionally on the way back to school at lunch time, I would walk beside him, and ask questions about the Civil War. I told him of my great grandfather, who also fought in that war and who was wounded when a piece of shrapnel hit him in the chest at the Second Battle of Bull Run.

On Memorial Day, we would travel in the family car to the home of my great aunt, my grandfather's sister. We would then go to the cemetery where they would plant geraniums on the graves of their parents.

There was always a flag in a G.A.R. veteran marker placed there by some veteran's organization. My grandfather's father had fought in the 4th Pennsylvania Reserves. After returning to my aunt's house for lunch, my grandfather would leave for some mysterious place called the "Post Hall".

My biggest thrill came when around ten or eleven years of age, I was considered old enough to accompany him on this journey. This was around 1932 or 1933. At that time, there were quite a few G.A.R. veterans left in Philadelphia. How exciting it was when I first entered Post #2 G.A.R. Hall at 667 N. 12th Street. What a magnificent building it was. The floor in the entry way was of white tile with a black design. To the right was the doorway to the library with its many books on the Civil War. On the left side was a stairway, divided by a landing, which went to the second floor. Among various Civil War mementos in the hallway was a cannonball embedded in a tree trunk fired during the battle of Chickamauga, and a ship's capstan from Admiral Farrragut's flagship, the Hartford.

From the hallway, one entered a large room with glass cases along the wall filled with relics from the Civil War. There was a large fireplace in the center of one wall over which hung a replica of a Grand Army badge, crossed swords, muskets, canteens, etc. There were captains' chairs with the names of Grand Army men who were members of the Post engraved on brass plates fastened to the chairs.

I was fascinated by a ship of bones on the mantel. a model made by prisoners in Libby prison. Eventually this model would disappear along with many other relics including several guns. As the neighborhood changed and the Grand Army was no longer around many lost interest. The building began to deteriorate. It was broken into several times and vandalized. Something had to be done about the situation. While the Grand Army no longer existed, the title to the building still had to be cleared. Since no one was doing anything, I stepped in and was given permission to take the necessary action. With the help of a lawyer from my church and after much work and difficulty, we eventually had the title cleared, and, with the help of a real-estate agent, the building was sold to a Negro Masonic Organization. With the help of Walt Mabie, President of the Corporation, relics were labeled, boxed, and put into storage.

Post 2 G.A.R. Memorial Hall
Philadelphia, PA

After several years with the help of Carl Gutekunst, the property on Griscom Street was purchased. Meanwhile Walt Mabie had died, but before his death, because of personal differences, I had resigned and transferred to another Camp.

To get back to the Post Hall, on the second floor was a hallway with a large office on one side and a storage room on the other. The hallway opened into a large auditorium where the Grand Army and the Sons and the Auxiliary met. The center of the room was carpeted in red. Benches on either side were elevated in tiers. In one corner of the room was a platform raised about 16 inches above the floor level and separated from the rest of the room by a brass railing. On the platform was a piano. It was here that a band sat during the Memorial Service. There were four stations of the Order with the Altar in the center. In front of the Commander's Station was a miniature canon in a glass case. Hanging on the walls were portraits of Civil War generals. To the right, hanging on the wall, was the mounted head of "Old Baldy", General Meade's horse which he rode during the war, and also the head of an Army mule. There were stacked muskets and drums at the front of the room. There were also two large brass cannons at the front of the room, one on either side of the Rostrum or Commander's Station. Regimental flags of the Union including that of Birney's Zouaves, along with the captured flags of the Confederacy were along the wall. Hanging from the ceiling of the room was a magnificent chandelier made of cannons, stacked muskets, and crossed swords, all in miniature. In a recess in the wall behind the rostrum or Commander's Station hung a large oil portrait of Abraham Lincoln along with various battle flags. On either side of the front, hung two large oil paintings, one of a Civil War soldier and the other of Union sailors.

There were still quite a few veterans living, relatively speaking, in those days. One of the veterans I remember in my early days was Colonel Samuel P. Town, an important member of the Grand Army, and the last surviving member of the original membership of Post #2. As the other posts in Philadelphia were disbanded, the remaining members would affiliate themselves with Post #2. In 1938, at the time of the "Blue and Gray" reunion in Gettysburg, there were only three G.A.R. posts left in the city. Post 1, Post 2, and Post 10. All met in Post Hall 2.

Colonel Town had enlisted as a private in the 20th Pennsylvania Cavalry in January 1864, at the age of 18, and had fought under Sheridan in the Shenandoah Valley campaign and with Grant at the close of the war in Petersburg. He had three cousins serving with the 95th Pennsylvanians, a Philadelphia regiment. At the battle of Salem Heights, a few days after the second battle of Fredericksburg, the 95th had every second officer and man killed or wounded ranking with the 20th Massachusetts as having the largest number of field and staff officers of any regiment killed or wounded. Among those was Colonel Gustavis W. Town who was killed, and Major Thomas J. Town and Lieutenant Samuel H. Town who were wounded. All three men were brothers.

Colonel Town was elected Commander-in-Chief in 1931 in DesMoines, Iowa, and presided at the 1932 Encampment in Springfield, Illinois. One of the things I remember about Colonel Town was his request that a hundred uniformed members of the Pennsylvania Brigade, Sons of Veterans Reserves be sent to Springfield as his escort. Money was raised and arrangements were made to fulfill his request. In those days, the Reserves were usually quartered at the local armory, although I never stayed there.

My first National Encampment was in 1939 at Pittsburgh; my second was in 1940 at Springfield, Illinois, and my third was at Columbus, Ohio in 1941. I next attended in 1946 at Indianapolis. I usually paraded with John Runkel's Harrisburg Fife and Drum Corp, and when John Runkle was elected Commander-in-Chief in 1950, he asked me to serve as his National Chaplain. I was privileged to attend the 75th reunion of the "Blue and Gray" at Gettysburg in 1938 which I shall write about later.

When I became old enough to join the Sons of Union Veterans of the Civil War, I also joined the Reserves, and was given a uniform and a rifle. Our Sergeant, Don Lewis, on one occasion made arrangements for us to have a practice drill before Memorial Day in a schoolyard in Frankford, a section of Philadelphia. I remember traveling by trolley and then the "El" from my home in southwest Philadelphia which took about an hour and a half in order to practice drilling to be ready for Memorial Day. In those days, the Reserves would hold an annual picnic at Willow Grove Park, an amusement park outside of Philadelphia. The various companies of the Reserves in Eastern Pennsylvania would compete in drilling and the winning company would be presented with a trophy. Members of the Grand Army would picnic with us.

On Memorial Day, I would get up early, put on my uniform, take my rifle and journey to the cemetery in South Philadelphia (Southwark) where the Reserves would assemble along with the Sons and Auxiliary and members of the Grand Army. We would visit two or three local cemeteries ending up at the cemetery of Old Swede's Church. I remember a watercolor painting done by someone of Comrade Henry F. Greenwood at Old Swede's Church cemetery. This painting used to hang in the G.A.R. Hall at 667 North 12th Street but has since disappeared.

Henry T. Greenwood had just turned 15 when he walked into the recruiting office of the 48th Pennsylvania Volunteers in Reading, Pennsylvania., and said that he wanted to enlist in the Union Army. The Irish Sergeant, he remembered, looked at him skeptically and asked, "how old are you son?" "Eighteen". he replied. The Sergeant winked at him and said, "Sure your heart's older than your face. Sign the papers here."

Colonel Samuel P. Town
Commander-in-Chief
1931 - 1932

A fife and drum corps of a Sons of Union Veterans unit photographed at Fifth and Capitol Avenue during the G.A.R. parade.
Springfield, Illinois, 1932

A group of veterans, stout of heart, but frequently with faltering step, as end of march neared.
Springfield, Illinois, 1932

A unit of Sons of Union Veterans marching with rifles over their shoulders led by drum corps.
Springfield, Illinois 1932

Officials on reviewing stand on courthouse square. Left to right in the picture: Congressman Richard Yates, Major John W. Kapp, Adj. Gen. Carlos E. Black, Col. H. Sheridan Baketel, Mrs. Samuel P. Town, and Commander Samuel P. Towne of the G.A.R.

G.A.R. Veteran Honors Dead Chief

Eighty-eight year old Henry T. Greenwood, commander of Post 71, Grand Army of the Republic is shown to the right, as he and Louis Herrmann, past commander of the Sons of the veterans, Camp 200, placed a wreath yesterday on the spot where the Commander-in-chief of the Northern forces in the Civil War - Abraham Lincoln - stood at Independence Hall.

Henry T. Greenwood

William H. Daily

His father was a corporal in the same regiment, and he spent the year of his enlistment, along with his father, on picket duty. When the year of his enlistment was up, young Henry left his father, and, on sudden impulse, joined the U.S. Marines. Shortly before the war ended, Henry started on a trip from the East to the West coast via the only water route available, around Cape Horn. The voyage was long and treacherous. For twenty-six months, his ship traveled through several storms, passing through a tornado on the way to the Cape and another on the western part of his journey. Many became ill, and considerable damage was done to the ship which had to be repaired. Henry's vessel finally touched San Francisco in 1867, and it was then that he learned the war was over. Back in civilian life, Henry resumed his job as an apprentice in a shoe factory. In time, he left his apprenticeship for other work. Eventually, he found work at the Philadelphia Navy Yard where he worked for 16 years, finally retiring at the age of 73.

To get back to Memorial Day, we would parade from Old Swede's Church up Delaware Avenue along old Dock Street(which is no more, but used to cover Dock Creek) to Independence Hall where the Grand Army would place a wreath on the spot where President-elect Abraham Lincoln stood to raise a new flag with thirty-four stars, the last being for the newly admitted state of Kansas. The Reserves were always the escort for the Grand Army. Here is a newspaper picture of Henry T. Greenwood, along with the members of the Reserves on one of those occasions. This ceremony is still continued by the Sons and the Auxiliary on Memorial Day.

After the ceremony, we would go by car to Post #2 G.A.R. Hall at 667 North 12th Street for lunch prepared by the ladies. After the lunch the old veterans would sit around conversing until it was time for the memorial service to begin. One of the veterans I remember was Zachary Kirk, a hundred day man. "Hundred Day Men", as they were called enlisted only for that length of time. He was one of 12,000 men called by Governor Curtin of Pennsylvania for a special emergency. It was feared that the Confederates were planning another offensive into Pennsylvania, and the Governor wanted to be prepared. Fortunately, this didn't happen, and so 18 year old Zachary Kirk went away in July 1864 to serve with the Western Army on the Mississippi. He returned in October 1864, having seen no major action, but bronzed and hardened with a military record which later enabled him to join the G.A.R. "They didn't look on us as cream-puff soldiers then", he said. "they were glad to have us and we were glad to go. We were glad to come back also". In spite of his limited record, Kirk was active in the GAR and held a number of offices.

Another old veteran that I remember was William H. Dailey who joined at age 17. He was learning the shoemaker's trade which he left to join the army. He walked down to the recruiting station and, before the month was over, headed for Lookout Mountain. Passing many plantations where there were still Negro slaves, they found the bodies of some Negro soldiers. "We were told that the Negro slaves were so frightened and angry that the war had been started, and were so afraid of what would happen to them that they shot down the members of their own race who were fighting to liberate them." When the 15th U.S. Infantry took over the mountain in November 1863, the Tennessee Valley was the chief theater of the war, and it looked as if the new soldiers would get a quick taste of battle. "We got orders to move to Knoxville cause word had come that the Confederates, who had lost that territory in September, were besieging the city. That was generally known as the second battle of Knoxville, and as it looked like it would be a long siege, we thought that we would soon see action." The siege was long, lasting from November 17th to December 3rd before the Confederates were beaten off and gave up the idea of retaking the city. But it did not mean action for Daily. "Just when we had everything packed and

Zachary Kirk

were waiting for marching orders, we received word not to go to Knoxville, but to stay on the mountain. I don't know why. The mountain was no longer any use to either side. But we stayed there, walking guard duty over nothing until we were transferred to Baltimore and Washington for more picket duty. I don't know how many miles I walked on picket duty in the war, but it was enough to earn me a long rest...."

How many veterans there were when I first began going to the Hall I really can't say. My impression is that there were quite a few. In 1937, there were seventy-five veterans left in Philadelphia, and in 1938, when I attended the Blue and Gray Reunion in Gettysburg, there were only 45 left in the city so you can see they were dying rapidly. I can see these men still leaning upon their canes, bent with age, wearing their starched white vests and their dark blue coats with their gold buttons and their Grand Army badges pinned to their coats. On their heads they wore the McClellan hat or kepi. In Pennsylvania, the Grand Army usually wore the McClellan Hat.

There were a couple of exceptions. One was William J. Baker who stood out not only because of his height (he was over six feet tall), but because he usually wore a white naval officer's hat. He was proud of the fact that he had served in the Navy. William J Baker had been born in England and was brought to this country at the age of six. Enlisting in the Union Army at the age of 15 - he was tall for his age - he served as a drummer boy during the battle of Gettysburg. After the battle, at the end of his enlistment, he joined the Navy and served under Farragut and Porter. He remembered the attack on Fort Fisher, North Carolina in 1864 and in 1865. Fort Fisher protected Wilmington, North Carolina which was a haven for blockade runners. While it was opened, British ships running the blockade could bring in supplies. General Lee warned Colonel William Lamb, Confederate commander of the fort, that it must be held at all costs for without the supplies from the blockade runners, his army could not be sustained. After a first attack on Fort Fisher in December 1864, failed, the Union General decided it could not be taken and withdrew. Meanwhile, the fleet of sixty vessels consisting of iron-clads, frigates, and gunboats rode out the winter gales at anchor. Colonel Lamb described it as "the most formidable armada the world has ever known."

Secretary of the Navy Wells insisted it was necessary to take the fort, and General Grant was ordered by President Lincoln to take it. In January 1865, after an assault by land as well as by sea, the fort was taken. The full fleet moved in close to the fort with its six-hundred guns and howitzers, and opened a cannonade to bring the fort into submission. Soldiers, sailors, and marines assaulted the fort and the last stronghold of the Confederacy finally fell. Baker was a gunner's mate and served on the screw-sloop Ticonderoga which held the left-end of the central line of three lines of warships. He said he would never forget the bombardment which, according to him lasted three days without ceasing. (Bruce Catton said two.)

After the war, Baker joined a ship's crew going to England. On his arrival in England, he joined the British Army and served nine years in India attaining the rank of Captain. On his return from India, he joined the London police force where he served twenty-five years as a London "Bobby". He said that when he was taking his examination for the London Police Force, they asked him about his military service. His answer was "Nine years in India, and three years in the American force during the late war". "With the south of course?" they asked, remembering that England had helped the Confederacy. "No sir, With the North of course." he replied, and they looked at him, swallowed hard, and went on with their examination. After the death of his wife, he returned to the U.S. where he remarried and continued to live off his Civil War and "Bobby" pension.

Another Naval veteran, I recall, was Henry Ziegler who was the last survivor of the naval battle of New Orleans and of the eventually successful attempt to run the Confederate batteries of Port Hudson, Louisiana. He served at the age of 18 as an ordinary seaman and was a shipmate of Lieutenant (later Admiral) George Dewey, who he met a number of times after his victory at Manila Bay. He also had the privilege of shaking hands with the "great Admiral David Glasgow Farragut".

Recalling the battle of New Orleans, he spoke of how in the early hours of April 24, 1862, after shells had bombarded the fort night and day, Farragut ran a gamut of severe fire and passed the two forts guarding the city, Fort St. Philip and Fort Jackson. The entrance to the city seemed impregnable. Ziegler's ship commanded by Captain Melancthon Smith was so near one of the Forts that he could hear the Confederate gunners swearing, "cursing Lincoln and praising Jefferson Davis for the benefit of the Yankees". His duty in battle was to help move the discharged guns back into position after firing. While the ship was often struck, they did good work on the forts.

Ziegler remembered when the Hartford, Farragut's flagship caught fire, "a calamity that nearly caused defeat for the northerners". Eventually, Ziegler's ship, the "Mississippi" was rammed by the Confederate ram, the "Manassa", and received a terrible gash. Then the Confederate ram ran ashore and under a fierce bombardment, her men fled into the woods to escape. Ziegler helped to move the guns that riddled her with shot and shell until she became a mass of flames. Ziegler was not wounded during this engagement, but fell against a gun and received a severe blow on the head which rendered him unconscious for a while.

He remembered the "din and thunder" of the battle and the spectacular appearance of a river full of fire. Farragut was to write home about it saying he wished his son could have seen it. It was here that Dewey won his laurels. He remembered the mad mob that greeted the ships as they came to New Orleans, and the quarrel between Farragut and the

Henry Zeigler

William J. Baker, 92
2338 Fitzwater St.

mayor about pulling down the "confederate flag". (It was really the flag of the state of Louisiana.) He said that Farragut threatened to bombard the city if they continued to fly the "confederate flag". Farragut finally had to send his own men to take it down as the local authorities refused to do it.

Ziegler also took an active part in the great event at Port Hudson. Port Hudson was located at a treacherous turn of the Mississippi. Her batteries were on a high bluff and her guns aimed at a point where the river was difficult to navigate. Port Hudson was the key to Vicksburg. This event which took place between the 15th and 16th, 1863, spelled disaster for his ship, the *Mississippi*, when it ran aground during the battle and had to be set on fire and abandoned. While the Hartford, Admiral Farragut's flagship, got through the other vessels were turned back. In recalling this event, Ziegler said it "was the greatest display of fireworks" he ever saw. When orders came to abandon ship, Ziegler nudged a friend of his who appeared to be leaning against a gun to follow him into the water only to discover that he was dead.

Captain Smith and Lieutenant Dewey remained on board their ship and were the last to leave. In leaving it, they set fire to their own ship. Ziegler was proud of the fact that before he leaped into the water to escape, he helped to fire the last gun on the "*Mississippi*". There were many casualties in the battle, and many of Ziegler's gun crew were killed. Rocked by explosion and burning the whole length, the "*Mississippi*" went down, and young able seaman Ziegler found himself in the river paddling with one arm, because the other arm was suddenly useless. He learned later, he had a ball through it. He was picked up by a union gunboat and after some weeks recuperating, he returned to duty. But for him the war was mostly patrol duty after that. There were no more Port Hudsons to capture.

Port Hudson itself was not taken until after Vicksburg had fallen. When the news of the surrender of Vicksburg was tossed into the fort, there came the shouted statement, "That's another damned Yankee lie". The battery finally capitulated on July 8, 1863.

Ziegler told an interesting story which was one of those experiences which could only be possible during the Civil War. A cousin of his had married a girl from Alabama, and when the war broke out, she insisted that he enlist in the Confederate Army which he did. He was taken prisoner at the Battle of Bull Run. He told the authorities that he was a northerner, and that his sympathies were with the union. He was released and enlisted in a Pennsylvania regiment. In July 1864, he was again taken prisoner this time by the Confederates at Cold Harbor. He was sent to prison, and was never heard from again by Ziegler or his family and friends. While he may have died in prison said Ziegler nobody knew what happened to him, and they felt that he may have been recognized by some of his former Confederate fellow soldiers and been shot for treason or desertion.

Ziegler served in the Union Navy for three years, and was the last surviving member of Post 10 of the G.A.R. in Philadelphia.

When it was time for the Memorial Service to begin people would assemble in the meeting hall. The old veterans would walk in together to take their seats on benches in the front of the room facing each other on either side of the rostrum. There was always a band present in the band section to play the National Anthem and other patriotic and Civil War music. Prominent men taking part in the service would sit on either side of the rostrum. Among other dignitaries would be the mayor of Philadelphia.

It was an impressive service. Among those who took part was the Reverend Elmer Finger, an inspiring speaker. Mr. Finger was called upon to speak at several memorial services as well as at Lincoln Banquets. The Reverend Mr. Finger was the pastor of the Dutch Reform Church at 15th and Dauphin

Streets in Philadelphia. Among his parishioners was Dennis E Casterlein. Dennis Casterlein was a New Jersey farmer boy who in 1864 ran away to join the Union Army at the age of 17. He and an older cousin first went to Pittston, Pennsylvania where he served bar for two weeks. ("I didn't know rum from whiskey," he said.) Then he went with his cousin to Philadelphia where he attempted to enlist, but was turned down when he admitted he was only 17. Then hopping a freight to Harrisburg, he was taken into the 194th Pennsylvanians when he said he was 18. He was given a make shift uniform because there were not enough to go around, and was assigned to Patrol Duty in the streets of Baltimore. From here, the 194th was ordered to Petersburg after the fighting. Then the 194th received orders to go on to Richmond. "We moved along the New Market Turnpike," he recalled, " to try to be the first to reach the city. But over to our right in the fields was a Negro regiment and we could see them running to get there first. It was a real race, we along the turnpike and they through the fields. We got there first and marched into the burning capital of the Confederacy" on April 3rd, 1865, a week before Lee surrendered to Grant at Appomattox Court House. He said he was "just one of the infantry men who tramped across the bridge into the city with my musket on my shoulders".

It was on Sunday, April 2, 1865 that word came to Jefferson Davis, while he was in church, that Richmond would have to be abandoned by nightfall. Panic swept the city. "The city had to be evacuated," he said, "and there was nothing to do but to take routine possession of the city." Richmond received the news that the end of the war was near. Lee's army had been broken at Petersburg and was in full retreat towards Danville. Jefferson Davis, President of the Confederacy assembled his cabinet and directed the removal of the seat of government, the archives, and the treasury to Danville. The residents of the Confederate capitol were thunderstruck by the news; they had felt entirely secured. They had to gather all their possessions for flight. All day wagons with their goods passed through the city. Somehow the city's arsenals were set on fire, perhaps deliberately, perhaps from stray shots. Magazine after magazine exploded. Bridges and building blazed. The earth shook. Mobs filled the streets and stormed commissaries of the fleeing army seizing food after months of war rationing.

As soon as the 194th arrived at Capitol Square and bivouacked , said Casterlein, "we stacked our arms and were told we were on fire fighting duty. The Engineers blew up houses and several streets to check the advance of the flames, and on the next day the fires were out". Dennis Casterlein was a harness maker by trade.

At the front of the hall, where we were gathered for the memorial service, there would be a vacant chair for each deceased comrade of the past year draped in black and placed in a row in front of the rostrum. When there were more members of the Grand Army of the Republic present, the Post Commander would ask,

"*Adjutant, for what purpose have we gathered?*"

The adjutant would answer, "To pay our tribute of respect to the memory of our late comrades."

Then the Post Commander would say, "Have you a record of their service in the cause of our country?"

The Adjutant would answer, "I have."

Then the Post Commander would say, "You will read it."

After each name and military record of the deceased was read there would be a roll of the drum as a comrade would slowly walk up and place a bouquet of flowers on a vacant chair. Then someone would sing "The Vancant Chair".

As they grew fewer in number, this would change. Here is part of an article which appeared in the Evening Public Ledger describing the event for Memorial Day 1939.

Private Casterlein in makeshift uniform (not enough uniforms to go around). Somebody stole his service cap.

Dennis C. Casterlein, 92
2209 N. Cleveland Ave.

"May 30th of '39 was a sad one for the two 92 year old warriors of the remaining eight who were able to attend the impressive ceremonies at Post 2, 667 N. 12th ST. This city's sole active G.A.R. headquarters now that the other posts have been\disbanded by death.

On that day Dennis C. Casterlien and Frederick J. McWade stood damp-eyed in the Post's vaulted assembly hall as first one and them another of five candles - one for each of their comrades - was snuffed out and a bouquet with a small American flag attached was placed on each of five empty chairs. Its always a question, of course, how many of the boys in blue would be able to turn out for the actual roll-call. John H. Liesee, a member of the Sons of Veterans and secretary of the post knew that.

Pondering over his records in his office, he said yesterday, 'H'mm, guess it narrows down this year to the most active three - that's Dennis C. Casterlein of 2209 N. Cleveland St., Frederick McWade of the Union League, and William Jackaway of 2621 Hutchinson St. The first two are 93 now, and Jackaway will be 100 in December, and they've been the most faithful at the regular meetings of the Post.'

These men I knew quite well. William Jackaway was born December 14, 1840. He was a volunteer fireman, and in 1861, enlisted in the 72nd Pennsylvanians which was composed of the Philadelphia Fire Zouaves known as Baxter's Fire Zouaves after their Colonel, D.W.C. Baxter and which was perhaps one of the most famous regiments in the Union Army. Their regiment was a part of the well known "Philadelphia Brigade". Since he was only 20 when he enlisted and the minimum age was 22, he grew a beard to make him look older. His father and two brothers also served in the Union Army.

Even before his regiment got into battle with the enemy, the Fire Zouaves ran into a harrowing experience. The regiment was moving along in the darkness, having just crossed Chain Bridge, Virginia, when it was fired upon by another body of men which they could not see. Although no Zouave was killed, many were wounded. There were also numerous casualties among the Philadelphia Cavalry and a California regiment, which, despite its name, was a Pennsylvania outfit, which was right behind them. It turned out that the firing was not done by the Confederates, but by the Philadelphia Irish Regiment. Somehow the Irish, who made up another famous local body of troops, had mistaken their compatriots for gray clad southerners and had opened fire on them without warning, an example of "friendly fire".

Jackaway served as a private for three years and ten days during which he was engaged in the thickest fighting of the war (31 major engagements). The 22 year old Jackaway was in the thick of the fighting at what he called the "Battle of Picket's Gap". Pickett's heroic but futile assault in the center of the union line is now history. Pickett survived, but Pickett's men were completely shattered. The brunt of the shattering was done in part by the Philadelphia Fire Zouaves, officially known as the 72nd Pennsylvanians, with the 22 year old Jackaway in the line. Jackaway recalled the confusion and carnage of the battle, their exhaustion afterward, and their care of the dead and wounded. There is a monument to this regiment at the "High Water Mark" of Picket's charge, a little to the right of the grove of trees.

When the regiment returned to Philadelphia on August 20, 1864, its original compliment of 1,500 men had been reduced to 210: 129 had been killed, 607 had been wounded, and 167 captured or missing. A contemporary account of their homecoming read, "they were met by members of City Council who escorted them to the Refreshment Saloon". Then the Zouaves paraded with the volunteer firemen and as they passed St. Peter's Church, the chimes played "Auld Lang Syne".

Jackaway died April 20, 1944 at the age of 103. I had the privilege of attending his 100th birthday celebration.

Monument to the 72nd Penna. Regiment at Gettysburg. William Jackaway served in this regiment.

William Jackaway

Samuel Hanson

After the memorial service at Post 2 Hall, we would march to the Post 2 Plot in Monument Cemetery at 15th and Berk Streets for a brief service. In earlier days some of the veterans would march with others, but later they would ride in cars. Today there is no more Monument Cemetery, and the ground is now a part of Temple University.

In 1938, I attended the 75th Reunion of the "Blue and Gray" in Gettysburg. At the time, I kept a brief account of my experience which I shall refer to later. During the Reunion I spent considerable time with three men from Philadelphia. One was Frederick J. McWade. Frederick J. McWade, as a student, had enlisted at the age of 17 in the 150th Regiment Ohio National Guard Infantry as a hundred day man. After being engaged in several skirmishes in Virginia in 1864, he was serving in Washington when Confederate General Jubal Early came swooping down upon the capital. Washington was encircled by a chain of forts which ranged along the opposite banks of both branches of the Potomac - a semi-circle of forts was to the north, the northernmost being Fort Stevens. Major General Alexander McD. McCook, who was without a command, was ordered to assume charge of the capitol's defense. McWade was at Fort Stevens when Early struck. Early expected to take the fort by surprise, but Fort Stevens and all the other fortifications, to his surprise, were fully manned.

"Early's heavy artillery was blasting away, and we were answering", said McWade. "That went on for three days and on the last day, President Lincoln came out from the White House with Secretary of State Seward to view the forts. They joined General Wright on the bombproof, and Lincoln stood erect despite the protestations of his aid. I can still see him", said McWade, " he was about seven feet tall with his hat. While Seward trotted along beside him, they urged him to get down, but he remained erect until a bullet dropped one of his

Frederick McWade,
Civil War veteran.
He saw Lincoln under fire.

staff, the surgeon. Then he bent down as if bewildered, and they moved back cautiously."

Mr. McWade never married and was attended at Gettysburg by his aid, Mr. Maurice Webb, who was employed as manager of the Appliance Department at Strawbridge and Clothier Department Store.

Comrade McWade was employed for forty years after the Civil War by the Pennsylvania Railroad as General Baggage Manager and was credited with organizing and perfecting the checking system of that railroad. He first served in its old office at 4th and Willing Alley before moving to Broad Street Station upon its completion. Now Broad Street Station no longer exists.

Mr. McWade lived in Holmesburg in his home in the summer, and moved to the Union League in the winter. He is buried in the churchyard of the Episcopal Church in Holmesburg where he served as vestry man for a number of years.

Another man who I knew rather well and who was at Gettysburg in 1938, was Samuel B. Hanson, who I called "Daddy Hanson". He was born March 15, 1842, in Manayunk. Philadelphia, and was mustered into the 15th U.S. Regulars (Infantry) on August 12, 1862, in Philadelphia at the age of 20. His father and four brothers all joined at the same time.

In the battle of Chickamauga, September 18-20, 1863, he was taken prisoner when a horse fell on him. He served seven months and eighteen days in Libby prison, and drew ration money for this period after his discharge. He weighed 198 pounds when he was taken prisoner and 98 pounds the day he was paroled. He was at Libby when the tunnel was dug, but he said, "the officers would not allow the privates through the tunnel". In Libby after the prisoners had dug the tunnel, and some had escaped, Mr. Hanson was moved to the tobacco factory across from Libby. When the Yankee gun boats got up the James River near Richmond, he was transferred to

Danville, Virginia. He was exchanged for a Confederate prisoner May 8, 1864, and was sent to Camp Chase, Ohio, rejoining his regiment in a few months.

After his capture at Chickamauga, he said, "I was glad to be out of the fighting for a little while", but the attitude soon changed. "Every day in Libby was a separate existence in hell," said Mr. Hanson. "The prison was so crowded that you couldn't take a deep breath without hitting some else in the ribs. There was practically no water; not enough to drink, let alone wash. I don't know how we survived it. After I rejoined my regiment, I was really after those Johnny Rebs with a vengeance, but the war is long over now, and there is no longer any more hard feeling." I visited Mr. Hanson, not only in Gettysburg and at the Post Hall, but at his home on East Venango Street, Philadelphia.

Two other men I knew slightly, and I mention them because their picture was taken along with two others in the Lincoln room at the Union League in Philadelphia. The comrade second from the left in the photograph is Charles L. Sherman who served in the First Connecticut Cavalry . Sherman enlisted at the age of 18 in New Haven, Connecticut. He saw service with the Army of West Virginia under Kilpatrick, Wilson, and then under the famous Custer. He, along with his outfit, was transferred to the Army of the Potomac where he "lived and swore by following the handle-bar mustache and the pert goatee of fighting Phil Sheridan". Across Virginia, the Army of the Potomac, commanded by General Meade, pursued General Lee and his tired Confederates. Sheridan's Cavalry and General Ord's Army of the James were pressing Lee's rear flank. Two nights before, by a lucky stroke, Sheridan had captured Lee's provision train upon which the Confederates were relying and forced the Confederates to halt for a day to scour the surrounding countryside for forage. Grant with his Union forces joined Sheridan's men at Appomatox Courthouse to

Lincoln Room
The Union League of Philadelphia
May 30, 1933
Charles L. Sherman (2nd from left)
Samuel S. Fowler (4th from left)

receive Lee's surrender. "Grant had been suffering from a headache for several days, I was told", Sherman recalled, " but as soon as he received Lee's message, his illness seemed to leave him".

This meeting took place in the home of Wilbur McLean, one of the villagers. Lee was waiting for Grant. The Confederate General sat at a small oval table, looking very fatigued. When the Union officers entered, they ranged themselves along the sides of the room very much as people enter a sick chamber when they expect to find a dangerously ill patient.

"General Grant's uniform, it was a private soldier's uniform except for the shoulder straps denoting rank, was spattered with mud. But General Lee had on a brand new uniform of Confederate gray. The Union officer asked his aide, Colonel Marshall, how it was that he and his chief wore such fine toggery. He explained that when their headquarters wagon was abandoned, and they found they would have to destroy all their baggage except the clothes on their backs, they naturally selected the best suits they had."

Here is another account, a southern view, which was given to me by a Confederate veteran, John H Sims who was from Texas and who was in Gettysburg in 1938. He served in the 13th Georgia Regiment of Gordon's Brigade, Stonewall Jackson's Corp.

"Grant said to Lee: 'For God's sake, let's quit butchering our men. You've killed 700 of my men this morning, and I don't know how many I have killed of yours. I have 150,000 men around you, and you have only about 7,000 men in all. You have nothing to fight me with. So, for God's sake, let's not fight anymore!" "Lee says, 'I will surrender on conditions,' and Grant says, 'Make your conditions, and I will accept them'. Lee says, 'I will surrender to you my guns, ammunition, and war material and nothing else.' Grant said,

Samuel S. Fowler

Charles L. Sherman

'I will accept', and whirled his horse and went back to Yankeedom".

We know that Lee's surrender was nothing like this, but I think it is an interesting account from a southerner's point of view.

The other man in the picture taken in the Lincoln Room, the fourth from the left, is Samuel S Fowler, who I knew. He was the Quartermaster General of the Grand Army at Gettysburg in 1938. He was also in charge of room 340 City Hall which, at one time, was the Grand Army Headquarters in Philadelphia.

Mr. Fowler was a sergeant-major during the Civil War, and served with the 34th Pennsylvanians for nearly three years. He was "never wounded, just scared". At Gettysburg, his regiment was assigned to guard the supply train between Emmitsburg and Gettysburg. There is a monument in Gettysburg to his regiment. His regiment started with an enlistment of 1,310 men and lost 750. Of these, 128 were killed in battle, 270 were wounded, 250 taken prisoner, and 102 died of disease and other causes.

After the war, Mr. Fowler was sent to North Carolina to establish a branch of his father's textile business and stayed there for twenty-seven years. While there, he was given a gold-headed cane by the Sunday School where he once served as Sunday School Superintendent. He called it his "Johnny Reb" cane. During the later years of his life, Mr. Fowler headed the Fowler Net and Twine Co. on Front Street in Philadelphia.

When I was seventeen years old, my grandparents took me to the 73rd National encampment of the Grand Army in Pittsburgh, Pa., August 27th to September 1st, 1939.

My second National Encampment was in Springfield in 1940, and my third in Columbus in 1941. While I had attended the 75th reunion of the Blue and Gray in Gettysburg the year before (1938), this was my first Grand Army Encampment. I

G.A.R. Veterans are assisted by Boy Scouts as they leave the reviewing stand for their seventy-third annual parade at Pittsburgh. Only two dozen at the 150 attending were strong enough to march.

will never forget arriving at the train station in Pittsburgh and meeting Horace and Molly Hammer. Horace was the Post Master of Reading, Pa. and the National Secretary and Treasurer of the Sons of Union Veterans of the Civil War. He had served continuously in this office from the time of his election in Gettysburg in 1905. Previous to this he had held the same office by appointment. Failing health forced him to submit his resignation in 1948. Horace was a short thin, bald-headed man with a round face and a cigar always in his mouth. He was a man of great energy and persistence.

After greeting us at the station, he insisted that we share a taxi ride to the Hotel. After piling our luggage into the taxi, there appeared not to be much room left for five people, but Horace was persistent that we could do it, and we all squeezed in. Horace told the driver where to go, and imagine our surprise when the Hotel turned out to be just around the corner from the station.

In those days, there were too many attending the encampment to stay at the same hotel. Needless to say, the Grand Army, along with the Woman's Relief Corp, always had first choice and would choose the best facility which in Pittsburgh was the William Penn Hotel. The Ladies of the Grand Army stayed at the Roosevelt. the Daughters at the Pittsburgher, and the Sons and Auxiliary took what was left, which in this case was the Fort Pitt.

One of the boys in the Reserves from Philadelphia had made a mistake in the date and had arrived some days earlier. He had hitchhiked from Philadelphia in his reserves uniform carrying his rifle and a brown paper bag with a few articles of clothing. He had five dollars in his pocket to cover his expenses. When he discovered his mistake, he headed for the nearest police station - downtown in the triangle. After explaining his predicament, he won their sympathy and they put him up at the police station until the opening of the encampment. They also took up a collection to help him with

Richard O. Partington
Pittsburgh, 1939

Richard O. Partington in front of Lincoln's home in Springfield, Illinois, 1940.

In front of Lincoln's tomb, Springfield, Illinois, 1940.
Richard O. Partington in Reserves uniform with his grandfather.

some of his expenses. His picture and story appeared in several newspapers including those in Philadelphia, and he became quite a celebrity and the recipient of the generosity of the good people of Pittsburgh. Needless to say he went home financially much better off than when he arrived.

Visitors began arriving, which included not only the members of the Grand Army and their attendants, but members of the Allied Organization, a large contingent of the Reserves, and members of the United States Marine Band under the direction of Captain Taylor Branson, along with their wives. The U.S. Marine Band, by an act of Congress, always attended the Grand Army Encampment where they would give several concerts and participate in the "Camp Fire" and the parade.

While members of the Reserve would usually stay at the local armory, I was fortunate enough to have my own room at the Fort Pitt Hotel paid for by my grandfather. I soon attached myself to John Runkle's Harrisburg Fife and Drum Corp. John, who eleven years later as Commander-in-Chief would appoint me his National Chaplain, graciously allowed me to march with the band playing the cymbals which required only banging them now and then with some semblance of rhythm.

In the evening, we would have what we called a "snake dance" or march through the downtown streets of the city. With the band leading the way, we would parade single file through the streets in and out of the various hotel lobbies and bars. People would line up behind us single file, strangers as well as members. Wherever we went, people would be laughing and singing and generally having a good time. I remember a man who obviously had a few drinks offering twenty dollars to allow him to bang on the bass drum. The band made twenty dollars that night. Ultimately, we would make our way back to the hotel where the band would continue to play. Rugs would be rolled back and people would dance. Someone from the band would put his hat on the floor,

Springfield, Illinois, 1940

Color Guard of the Sons of Union Veterans Reserves

U.S. Marine Band before parade

Two unknown veterans being escorted through New Salem, Illinois
Springfield, Illinois, 1940

Grand Army Men marching in the parade at Columbus, Ohio in 1941.

A. A. Gage
Columbus, Ohio, 1941

Richard R. Graham of Madisonville, Kentucky, Accompanied by his son Columbus, Ohio, September 1941

Jacob Mooker of Valpariso, Indiana
Columbus, Ohio, 1941

and people would make donations to help the Reserves with their expenses. No one bothered us, and all seemed to be having a good time. Of course, there were many young people with lots of energy.

The hotel lobbies were crowded, especially the William Penn with the Grand Army men sitting in the lobby. They were always the center of attention and seemed to be enjoying themselves. There was a piano in the lobby, and every now and then, someone would sit down and begin playing. People would gather around and begin singing. I remember one afternoon a young man with a beautiful voice leading the singing. We soon found out he was Lanny Ross, a popular radio singer at the time, who was known as the "Street Singer".

Of course, I was not permitted to attend the Grand Army meetings which were usually of short duration. In order to deal with the Grand Army, one had to go through the National Secretary of the Grand Army, Katherine "Kitty" Flood (later it was Cora Gillis).

A controversy developed - believe it or not - over the motion picture "Gone With the Wind". A resolution by Thomas Ambrose, a Grand Army man, was adopted. The resolution charged the picture from the book, depicting life in Atlanta during the "war between the states" portraying the Union soldiers as "a hideous marauder attacking women" and urged that the "G.A.R. absent themselves" from any theater showing "this defamatory film".

Since the Grand Army membership and influence had considerably declined through deaths, with only 150 attending this encampment, their resolution was ignored. Mrs. Edna R. Carroll, chairwoman of the Pennsylvania Board of Motion Picture Censors, said that "the controversy would have no influence on them". "I read the book," she added, " and it left me with a definite feeling that the invading states were held up in a bad light. I was not particularly happy because it was 'a reflection on the north. But that's history. That's what happens in war. I don't think there in any basis for banning a picture on those grounds. From advance notices, I still think the picture will be a treat. I hope this doesn't get us involved in another Civil War."

Robert N. Rownd of Ripley, New York, was Commander-in-Chief. Robert N. Round was a short, rather plump man with a full face and who stood and sat as straight as a "ram-rod". He wore pince-nez glasses and had a high starched or celluloid collar. He had a full head of hair which I was never able to decide if it was his own or a hairpiece. Commander Round was 95 years old at the time, and died at 104 in his home in Ripley, New York.

Robert Rownd was born in Sarahsville, Ohio, and had volunteered for service in the 27th Ohio Volunteers as a drummer boy at the age of 17. His parents objected and obtained his release. Running away from home, he tried to enlist again, but was turned down because of his age. On the third attempt, with his parents finally consenting, he was successful. He served with Company B of the ninth Ohio Volunteer Cavalry, and was in sixty-six engagements, and in General Sherman's march from Atlanta to the sea. Mr. Rownd served two terms as Commander-in-Chief, in 1939 and again in 1947. He received a diploma from Allegheny College in Meadville, Pennsylvania, sixty-five years after he had left college to fight in the Civil War.

John Andrews, who succeeded Robert Rownd as Commander-in-Chief and who died in office, had a interesting story which he told. In 1889, he attended the Grand Army Encampment in Milwaukee, Wisconsin where he met General Sherman on the street. After saluting, he said, "General, I was one of your boys on the march to the sea". General Sherman, after greeting Comrade Andrew cordially, slowly replied, "No doubt you were. But I had only 75,000 boys with me on that march, and I have already met over 200,000 of them."

John E. Andrew
Commander-in-Chief
Died in office, June 30, 1940

Robert M. Rownd
Commander-in-Chief
Pittsburgh, 1939

There were many activities going on at the National Encampment. Briefly, on Sunday evening, there was a memorial service for the veterans of the Grand Army who had passed away during the year. This was lead by the Reverend Joshua A Pierce of Denver, Colorado, a Grand Army man who was "Chaplain -in-Chief". Wednesday evening was the Grand Army campfire held in the Soldiers and Sailors Memorial Hall. On Thursday evening at Flag Staff Hill, Schenley Park, there was a pageant depicting Civil War days. During the week, the United States Marine Band, under the direction of Captain Taylor Branson, and which was always present at Grand Army Encampments, gave concerts from 7:30 P.M. to 8:00 P.M. at the Soldiers and Sailors Memorial Hall.

There was always a parade in the Encampment City, the center of which was always the Grand Army. While there were 150 members of the Grand Army in attendance at the Encampment, only two dozen felt strong enough to march in the parade. Imagine what a thrill it was to see these grand old men marching, the remnant of what was once a great army. The Sons of Veterans Reserves were always the escort for the Grand Army. The Marine Band, along with members of the Pennsylvania National Guard, and the Boy Scouts, etc. were all in the parade. After the parade, we would march back to the hotel and line up in the mezzanine where we would receive a few dollars in so-called "military pay".

One evening, members of the Reserves along with several young ladies attending the Encampment were invited by Ruth Hawk, a member of the Ladies of the Grand Army of the Republic to a barn dance at her farm. We went in several cars. Ruth supplied the refreshments, including bottles of soda kept in several galvanized tubs containing large pieces of ice. We danced until the "wee hours" of the morning. When I got back to the hotel, I received a scolding from my grandfather who was worried about me.

I attended several sessions of the Sons in the Hotel ballroom. The room was filled with members. The Commander-in-Chief of the Sons was William Anderson of Massachusetts. His project was trying to promote the G.A.R. highway bill through the various state legislatures. This was difficult because the Spanish American War Veterans were promoting the name of Theodore Roosevelt for the highway. In time, the G.A.R. highway bill was passed by the various state legislatures so that the Grand Army Highway would run from the Atlantic to the Pacific.

The encampment in 1939 was from August 27th through September 1st. Many would arrive a day or two before and usually leave a day or two after. In returning home on September 1st on the train, I remember a newsboy going through the train selling his newspapers and shouting the headline, "Germany Invades Poland". Thus as I left my first encampment of the Grand Army of the Republic. I was conscious of those who had fought in one war, and wondered if we would eventually send our men to fight in another. These are some of my reminiscences of my association with the Grand Army of the Republic and other veterans of the Civil War, for not all Civil War veterans were members of the Grand Army of the Republic. While at Gettysburg, I learned that one of the veterans from the area had gone home because of illness. While not a member of the Grand Army, Mr. Webb and I later visited him at his home in Ridley Park, PA. He was Christopher C. McCullough. Mr. McCullough was born December 25, 1842, on a farm in Rising Sun, MD. He was working on his father's farm when he enlisted as a volunteer at Fort Deposit, MD, on August 14, 1862, at the age of 19. He enlisted in the 6th Maryland Regiment, 2nd Brigade, 3rd Division, 6th Corps. he served with the same regiment until his discharge on June 20, 1865, in the Shenandoah Valley. He was a corporal at the time of his discharge. He was present at Lee's surrender, and then was sent to the Shenandoah Valley.

After the battle of the Wilderness, where he was slightly wounded in the right shoulder by a "spent ball", he was captured and taken to Richmond, and placed in Libby Prison. His health was so poor that he became sick with Typhoid Fever. He was taken to the hospital, but he forgot where because the fever caused him to be unaware of his surroundings. He was later paroled, and rejoined his regiment.

I want to mention in closing Comrade Alfred W. Gabrio, who was the surviving member of the Grand Army in Pennsylvania. Comrade Gabrio was a "hundred day man". His father was a veteran of the Mexican War.

Comrade Gabrio was born February 3, 1846 at White Haven, Luzerne County, Pennsylvania. Immediately preceding the outbreak of the Civil War, the family located on a farm in Genesco, IL. In 1861, his father and three brothers enlisted in the Union Army, leaving young Alfred, who was only 15, at home with his two sisters.

At 17, he enlisted, but his mother, claiming he was under age, obtained his release. Later, with his mother's consent, he enlisted in Co. K, 139th Illinois Infantry, and was mustered in on June 1, 1864. The 139th participated in the Mississippi and Red River campaign. He helped in clearing the Red and Yazoo Rivers and Island No. 10 - mostly fighting guerrillas. In 1945, the Union League in Philadelphia, along with Comrade Gabrio paid tribute to Abraham Lincoln on Lincoln's Birthday with ceremonies in the Lincoln Room. At the time, Dr. Robert C. Clothier,, the President of Lincoln University, was the speaker. I mention this because, about 15 years later, I was the speaker on a similiar occasion, speaking on Lincoln's visits to Philadelphia. I was privileged to attend Comrade Gabrio's 100th birthday observance.

In 1949, taps were sounded for the last time by the Grand Army of the Republic as it passed out of existence. Their story has been forgotten by a nation which no longer remembers nor honors its past. It belongs to another time,

Alfred Wiles Gabrio

1846 - 1946

A puff on his Perfecto makes Alfred W. Gabrio, 99 commander of the Pennsylvania Department, Grand Army of the Republic, reminiscent of his old Commander-in-Chief, Abraham Lincoln, whose 136th birthday anniversary is celebrated today.

Greeting his Second Century with Song

Alfred W. Gabrio, of Hazelton, Pennsylvania, Department commander of the Grand Army of the Republic, raises his voice in a Civil War marching song at a testimonial dinner in honor of his 100th birthday. At right is his daughter, Mrs. Alverna Scott. Standing is Frank Heacock, Sr., of Perkasie, state commander of Sons of Union Veterans.

another era, which, too frequently I feel, applies to me, but they were an important part of my boyhood and my youth. I cannot help but think that, with the passing of the Grand Army of the Republic, something precious has passed from the American scene, and we, as a people, are poorer for it. In my study, I have a framed page taken from "The Ladies Home Journal" dated June 1939. It is a picture of a painting by Norman Rockwell. It portrays an empty chair with a G.A.R. hat on the seat and a cane resting against it. Lying at the foot of the chair is a dog with an expression of sadness. In the background are various figures of young men and boys marching in their uniforms of various shades of faded blue.

I have never seen a print of this picture since. While visiting the a Norman Rockwell Museum in Stockbridge, MA recently, I inquired about this painting, but no one seemed to know it. There was, however, a catalogue (which was not for sale) of all of Norman Rockwell's paintings. There it was, listed as privately owned. Perhaps this is why copies are not available.

Underneath the painting was a poem by McKinley Kanter entitled "The Death of the G.A.R.". This poem expresses my sentiments in relation to my experience of the passing of the Grand Army of the Republic.

The Death of the G.A.R.
(A Rhyhme for Memorial Day)

By McKinlay Kantor

Now they are gone from Webster City.
Mr. Lee was the last to go
Coffin damp with the snowball's snow,
Coffin damp with the lilacs' pity).
E. N. Lee was the last to go
To narrow quarters with flag above,
And the soft tattoo of the mourning dove....
He lies at ease in the burying ground,
While a comrade tells of his Vicksburg wound.

And another mutters of Malvern Hill
Or Shiloh Church or Andersonville,
Musket or tent or rebel shout -
But the tardiest soldier is mustered out.
They are gone, they are gone, and more is the pity
For the great-grandchildren of Webster City.

Daughters and sons of the chromium age,
Grasp this moment, and hold this page,
And let me describe the homely ration
That fed the belly of half our nation.
There was something about them you cannot know -
But it lived before you began to grow,
And it made the soil that we rear you in.
(The shrill machines have shredded it thin.)
It was sweet as maple and gold as wheat
And it lived in every Northern street;
It gave us manna we cannot give
No matter how long God lets us live.

It is past, it is vanished and cut clean off,
And only a relic stays to cough
And remind us all of the sundry riches
We stowed in our early childhood niches.

This story stemmed from a buggy wheel
And a pacing mare and a shaving mug
And the keen straight edge of a razor's steel,
And it lived in every tobacco plug -
In an argument in the courthouse yard -
In the horehound candy at Kearn's store,
In cubebs and lanterns and buckets of lard -
In the lovely things that are here no more,
The things we thought were ugly before.

I am talking about the G.A.R.,
That some of you think is a big bronze star
Kept in a desk that grandpa used,
And by worthy sentiment thrice-abused.
But the G.A.R. was more than that -
More than a cord on a battered hat -
More than a ghost or a rural fairy
That sleeps up there in the cemetery.

It was stuff that we who witness its death
Will miss as long as God gives us breath:
The frosty cheek and the black molasses,
And the fudge that grandfather always stole -
And where did you put my fishing pole?
And hurry along to your Sunday-school classes! -
The Templar charm and the celluloid collar,
The Cross of Gold and the silver dollar -
And Teddy will run for another term.
And I won't support Bill Bryan again.
And I was always a Cleveland man!
Here lay the ripe dissension's germ,
But all forgotten and washed away
Whenever the Comrades met in May.

We count the tracks of the tribal old

Over the windy ridge of time
Through fire that burned on a Piltdown wold
To the first man stirrings within the slime.
There is worship for Chinese ancestors,
There is blessing for elder sainted monk . . .
Shall we who gazed at the harness stores
Lock our past in a haircloth trunk?

Partly legend and partly lie,
And partly pure as the Maytime sky -
This was the Army that we had.
It was saved and shriven and could not die,
And it had a song that would drive you mad:
Limping under the shade of oak
With picket fences to hem it in,
Its drummers beat and its fifers spoke
(And the beard grew out of the shrunken chin).
The song of the Army comes to mind
Telling the tale we never find
Now that the drums no longer din . . .
These are the things that we will miss:
The big bear hug and the whiskery kiss,
The room with a sagging, painted shutter,
The asthma sound, and the midnight mutter,
And the trousers hanging across a chair,
And the thought that grandfather sleeps in there -
The Odd Fellow pin and the Indian story,
And the grave in Washington Territory.
Sons and daughters of radio,
E. N. Lee was the last to go!
You knew not him or his shaggy brother
But they were kinder than many another.
Wesley Martin and George S. Neel -
They were a dream you cannot feel. . . .
Captain Landers and Parker Banks -

Gone to manage the mystic ranks. . . .
Sons and daughters, award your thanks
To the black cigars and the oyster suppers,
To the coffee mills and the leather cruppers
And all of the worn American treasure
That you and your age can never measure.

Now they are gone from Webster City
And most of the other towns as well.
Daughters and sons, to you our pity,
For we have a story you cannot tell.

Chapter II
Gettysburg, The 75th Reunion - 1938

In 1938, I attended the 75th reunion of the "Blue and Gray" in Gettysburg. What an exciting time that was. Eighteen hundred old men encamped in a modern electrified tent city for three days. Here they met on the ground of their greatest battle and their reunion for the last time on earth.

To accommodate these old veterans, the government erected 3,800 neat brown tents, installed ten miles of plumbing and twenty miles of electrical wiring, dropped 50,000 yards of mosquito netting, provided hundreds of wheel chairs, and five cases of whiskey. When the whiskey ran out after two days, a plane was sent for two cases more.

Some Confederate veterans, anticipating the reunion, expressed concern over whether or not they could wear replicas of their Confederate uniforms or display their Confederate flags. One of the northern veterans express the fear that "there will be trouble in camp if there are any Confederate flags". Another veteran, in expressing concern, followed this with the suggestion that "they had better put all the liquor out of the camp or the boys may cause trouble". In spite of this concern, however, every thirsty veteran was served a toddy containing a small amount of whiskey (dram or 1/8 ounce). One bearded centurion demanded more than was being served.

The fears expressed were more than offset by the expressions of most. "Thank God, time has healed the passions" or "we are now all one country" or they "looked forward to meeting their former foes and shaking their hands". Needless to say, the southern veterans wore replicas of their Confederate uniforms and flew their Confederate flags and liquor was kept to a minimum. Evidence of the spirit of these old veterans was the suggestion of some that they stage a sham

Announcement at Gettysburg,
PA Corner

Eternal Light Memorial . . .shall beckon . . .where once this cannon roared

To each veteran...a soldier is assigned...to hear old tales ...and help.

There were no floors...under Union tents...75 years ago.

Old wounds are healed . . for "Yank" and Confederate" alike . . In amity they will return to Oak Ridge. . . and Little Round Top

Taps over Gettysburg brought slumber to 1,300 veterans in the Union Army encampment, 500 in Confederate tent city (left). Each old soldier had his own tent.

Wheel chairs were provided for all veterans unable to walk. No veteran died during the reunion. Only 40 had to be sent home, most of them for homesickness.

battle at the reunion for the benefit of the public, proving that while the spirit was willing, the flesh was weak.

Medical officers marveled at the excellent health and spirits of these oldsters whose average age was 94. On July 4th, after a strenuous day of fireworks, oratory, and army maneuvers, only 32 hospital beds were occupied. One patient, who was 104, was suffering from alcoholism.

At the time of the reunion, I kept a brief account of my experiences along with various interviews which Maurice Webb and I had with several old veterans. The pictures I took were rather poor as I am not a photographer, but, thanks to my daughter, they have been greatly improved with the computer.

June 29, 1938 - Arrived in Gettysburg, and registered at the Hotel Gettysburg. Today the first veterans arrived by train. They are being transported by bus to the tented city north of town.

Washed and went out to look over the town. There are many decorations and the store windows have Civil War relics. The town is very small and there seems to be very few people on the streets. Perhaps this is because I expected more.

Went to movies this evening.

June 30 - More people seem to be arriving all the time. The little town is becoming very crowded and appears to be busy.

I went out to the tent city where the northern veterans are encamped. Things are very nice out there. There are boardwalks all over the tented city which connect the various tents so that men can walk easier or be pushed in wheelchairs easier. There are many wheelchairs with veterans in them, being pushed by boy scouts. The veterans from Philadelphia are coming in, and among them are comrades Kirk, Hanson, Fowler, and

This picture was taken on our way to the dedication by President Franklin D. Roosevelt. I am on the left.

Two members of the S.V.R. were with me. Again, I am on the left.

Jackaway. (Zachary Kirk - was "Hundred Day" man served with 197th Pa. Vol.; Samuel Hanson - served with the 15th U.S. Infantry, served 7 months in Libby Prison; Samuel S. Fowler - served in the 84th Pa. Vol., is now Quartermaster General of the G.A.R.; William Jackaway - served with the 72nd Pa.-Phila. Fire Zouaves and was in the Battle of Gettysburg.) During the day, I spent much time with them, especially "daddy" Hanson.

July 1 - The opening services were held today at the College Stadium. Governor Earle of Pennsylvania is here. More people seem to be arriving all the time. Visited the camp. Enjoyed getting into groups where the veterans were telling stories of the Civil War.

July 2 - The parade was held this afternoon. We were busy eating lunch in the dining room of the Hotel Gettysburg. Everybody would jump up at one time or another to watch the parade. Among those in the dining room was General Smedley Butler of the U.S. Marine Corps. He wasn't in uniform. Every once in a while a young woman would jump up to look at the parade, and would say, "Come here, Father." Then the General would get up and go over to the window and watch. My grandfather knew him from his days as Director of Public Safety in Philadelphia. He went over to talk with him, and it was then I met him.

This evening the town seems to be wild with excitement. Part of the Army and the National Guard is here, also members of the Marine Band, and lots of Boy Scouts.

Walking around the center of town, I ran into two fellows I knew from Philadelphia. They had their Reserve uniforms on. They had hitch-hiked up to Gettysburg on five dollars. This was all they had. I went back to my hotel room and changed into my uniform, and then we went roaming through the streets. When it got late, I took these two fellows out to the northern camp, succeeding in getting them, through the help of a National guard Officer who was a member of the Sons, into an empty tent. The soldier assigned to that tent was from Philadelphia, and had gotten sick and gone home.

July 3 (Sunday) - Went out to the camp and found my two friends had gotten their breakfast, free of charge, at the mess tent along with the Veterans. We visited the Battlefield, and the Army Camp. I then visited Comrades Kirk and Hanson and Fowler (Fowler being a Nat'l Officer of the G.A.R. was in the first section of the camp), and roamed around the streets of the Tent City stopping to talk to some of the Veterans. I had a pass and could get into the camp any time I wanted.

At five o'clock (P.M.), we started out for the Peace Memorial. On the way, many people stopped us to take our pictures in our Reserve uniforms. Many ladies asked if they could be photographed with us. Of course we consented. There was a big wooden platform covered by canvas. Here were the seats for the Veterans, their aides, and government officials. At about three or four feet a rope was strung all around the stand. This was to keep back the crowd which was as far as the eye could see. (The newspapers estimated that there were 200,000 people there that day.)

Between the stand and the rope holding back the crowd were state policeman patrolling the area. We walked right through the crowd, under the rope and past the state police, who never said a word, right up to the stand and sat down. Some of the people standing in the crowd stared at us in amazement. We had a good view

Mess Hall where my two friends ate.

Mess Hall
J. F. Howell (without beard) and his young wife

McWade

McWade ... second from right
Webb ... far right

Three Veterans Sitting
Dr. Mennet on right (two unknown)
Gettysburg, 1938

Lincoln Impersonator
with part of a
photograph
of another Lincon
impersonator

Lincoln Impersonator
Gettysburg, 1938

of all the speakers and could hear them all plainly, including the President of the U.S.(Roosevelt). After the dedication, the President and Governor Earle left by the road behind the stand where we were. We went to the rear and saw them plainly as they passed by a few feet from us, waving as they passed.
We then met Comrade McWade from Philadelphia, who was with his attendant, a Mr. Webb. During the summer Mr. McWade lived at his home in Holmesburg, but in the winter months he moved to the Union League. (Frederick McWade served with 150th Ohio and remembered seeing Abraham Lincoln on his visit to Fort Stevens in 1864.) The comrade wanted to see the Memorial from close range so, assisted by a State Trooper, we went through the crowd up to the Memorial. We then had our pictures taken with Comrade McWade. Then we went with Comrade McWade and Mr. Webb to the army display. Had a police escort. Again we managed to get a seat.

July 4 - Met my two friends (including Comrade McWade and Mr. Webb) and went to the U.S. Army demonstration. We met a Confederate veteran who invited us to have lunch with him at the Confederate Mess Tent, which we did. The veterans are starting to leave today.

This afternoon Mr. Webb and I went around the camp taking pictures and writing interviews which we had with the veterans. While talking to an old veteran, a newspaperman, I believe, from Danville, Ind., came up and took my picture with the southern veteran, a very interesting man, General Paul Savguinette, Adjutant General, Alabama Division U.C.V.

General Savguinette, the gentleman with whom my picture was taken, was born on September 6, 1846, at Bathia, Corsica, France ("in the same town and on the

R. O. Partington with Confederate veteran, Paul M. Sanguinetti from Alabama.

same island as Napoleon"). In 1859, he came to Richmond, Virginia, on a visit to his uncle and cousin. While there, war broke out and he enlisted. He was mustered into the 19th Virginia Infantry in the spring of 1861. He took part in the Seven Days fighting around Richmond in 1862, and was under Lee at his surrender at Appomatox Court House, Va., in 1865, "after being three days with nothing to eat". After the surrender, he returned to Richmond with "nothing but the dirty, ragged uniform he had worn for four years". He then became a store clerk in a grocery store. A friend from Montgomery, Alabama, learned from returning soldiers that Mr. Savguinette was in Richmond. He sent his brother to get him. He bought a new suit of clothes, and went to Montgomery. They had no sidewalks and everything was mud.

Mr. Savguinette's only wound was when he was in the front ranks of the infantry. They were resisting a cavalry attack at Dreury's Bluff. A saber cut off his right thumb when he held up his gun to protect his head.

July 5 - Comrade McWade, Mr. Webb, and my two reserve friends left today, and I will follow them tomorrow thus marking the end of one of the most memorable experiences of my life.

William H. Jackson, Union Veteran (left), and Robert H. Wilson, Confederate veteran (right), discuss their experiences in the war as they drop flowers on the battlefield in Gettysburg in 1938.

John M. Claypoole
Commander-in-Chief
of
U.C.V.

Governor William W. Scranton

and

The Gettysburg Centennial Commission

request the honor of your presence

at

The Ceremonies

in commemoration of

The 100th Anniversary of

Lincoln's Gettysburg Address

Tuesday, November nineteenth

Nineteen hundred and sixty-three

Gettysburg, Pennsylvania

R.S.V.P.

Invitation sent to Richard O. Partington on the occasion of the 100th Anniversary of The Gettysburg Address

William Barnes

The next picture is of a veteran I met named, William Barnes, who lived at 943 Cypress Street, Oakland, California. In a picture book entitled "Hands Across the Wall", he is identified as an "unidentified Negro veteran". I mention him because I met him in Gettysburg in 1938. He was born December 25, 1826 at Lexington, Kentucky, which, at the time of the reunion, would have made him 111 years old. Because of his age it was difficult to talk to him, but he did tell me he was born a slave and ran away from his master in order to serve with the "Yankees". He was in the U.S. Artillery, and served for 2 years. He was wounded twice, both times at Gettysburg. "They got me with a sword," he said, "and shot me in the hip."

Rudolph A. Becker

Rudolph A. Becker, Minnesota Soldier's Home and Hospital, Minneapolis, Minnesota.

He was born in Germany on January 5, 1848, and mustered into the service about August 1, 1862, at Milwaukee, Wisconsin. He fought at Gettysburg in the 26th Wisconsin V.I. His first fight was at Chancellorsville "where we got licked". He had been at Fredericksburg, but didn't get into the fighting. "There Franz Sigel would not take his troops into the fighting as it was slaughter."

Dilger's Battery was on Mr. Becker's left at Gettysburg, he recalled, in the first day's fighting. After the repulse north of town, he recalls his regiment being stationed at a toll gate across a road at the edge of Baltimore Pike on Cemetery Hill. He couldn't speak one word of English until he got up around headquarters. The officers spoke German and gave all their orders in German.

B. F. Red

In 1938, Comrade McWade, who I had mentioned previously, his attendant, Maurice Webb, and B.F. Red, a Confederate veteran, a Mrs. Bell, and another veteran had their picture taken in back of a sign reading the McMillan House.

Mr. B. F. Red lived in the Arkansas Confederate Home. He was born in Hendersonville, North Carolina, but left there as a boy and was raised in Clarksville, Georgia. He was mustered into the Confederate Army, June 11, 1861, near Big Shanty, Georgia, in Company "C", Phillips Legion where he remained throughout the war. He fought in the Army of Northern Virginia in Woffard's Brigade, Kershaw's Division, Longstreet's

He was wounded three times during the war, one of which was at Antietam.
At Gettysburg, Woffard's Brigade consisted of Phillips Legion, Cobbs Legion, the 16th, 18th, 24th Georgia regiments. Before he charged at Gettysburg on July 2nd, they got into the basement of a farmhouse, and got into some apple butter. They charged, reached the base of Little Round Top, were repulsed, retreated, and then went back for more apple butter. He stopped at a farmhouse on July 3rd, 1938, with his attendant when he recognized the doorway leading to the cellar. The young woman in the photograph, a Mrs. Myrtle D. Bell, is the great grand-daughter of David McMillan who lived in the house at the time of the battle.

Frederick McWade
(2nd from left),
B. F. Red
(2nd from right),
Myrtle D. Bell
(end on right)

F. Scott Dance
Towson, Maryland

Born January 5, 1843, in Delaneys Valley, Baltimore County, Maryland

Mustered in a week or two after Battle of Antietam. Ran through the blockade at night to enter Richmond. Then got over to New Market, Virginia, to get in the 1st Maryland Cavalry, C.S.A.

General Jones took the troops into West Virginia to raid - his first engagement of any consequence.

Was at Gettysburg under General Early. Was among the last to cross the Potomac River at Williamsport on the retreat. Had to swim horses part way across stream

Elbridge S. Fenton
4099 Howe Street, Oakland, California

He was born in Canton Township, Bradford County,
   Pennsylvania, November 22, 1846. Mustered into
   service in September, 1863, and mustered out in June,
   1865.
Fought at Gettysburg - the first major fighting he was in. Got
   to Frederickburg a week or two after the battle. Was at
   Chancellorsville in the 5th Corps, but saw no fighting.
   Was in the 12th Pennsylvania Reserves at Gettysburg -
   got there the night of the 2nd day. Had marched 3 days
   forced marched to get there from Arlington Heights
   below Washington. Was thrown into position behind
   another regiment as reserves. Doesn't recall what he

did at Gettysburg except he just followed orders. Did some fighting on the third day.

After the battle of Gettysburg, he was in Veterans Reserves Corps, whose function it was to guard recruits until enough were in a company to send to the front.

He had a brother, Edgar Fenton, who was in the same regiment, same company. Brother Edgar was in Libby prison for six months, fourteen days. He died ten years ago.

Alfred F. Fuller
R 1, Duback, Louisiana

Born March 3, 1848, Union Parish, Louisiana. Mustered into service February 1, 1963 - not quite 15 years old - near Vianna, Louisiana in Company "E" of 12th La. Infantry. First gun was fired at Bentonville, La. Never wounded, he had his clothes shot off a time or two. Was at Champion Hill and Baker's Creek. Was under General Joseph Johnston on his retreat before Sherman's march into Georgia. After the fall of Atlanta Wood's army retreated to Franklin, Tennessee. Surrendered with General Joseph Johnston in North Carolina. Liked Johnston but didn't like Hood because he was not careful of his men. Mr. Fuller fought at Kenesaw Mountain. Mr. Fuller's picture taken with his arm around Mr. McWade was on the 1st page of the Baltimore Sun, Friday June 30, 1938. He was in Loring's Division throughout the war.

O. Richard Gillette
Commander, Louisiana Division, U.C.V.
205 Court House Building, Shreveport, Louisiana

Born September 23rd, 1845, in Suka, Mississippi
Mustered in April 30, 1861, in Co. K, 2nd Mississippi Infantry.
   Helped Private Powell of Louisiana Tigers with General Stonewall Jackson's horse many times. Was on Jackson's staff.
Was on Picket's left during the charge at Gettysburg on 3rd day.
Fought under Longstreet at Battle of Wilderness. had 175 rounds of ammunition and 3 hands full of parched corn in morning and only 3 rounds of ammunition at end of day. Got tired of picking off Northerners from the hill.

Northerner's didn't know how to shoot in the thick underbrush. Neither side could use artillery at the Wilderness because of undergrowth.

John W. Harris

20th Tennessee Cavalry
Bell's Brigade
Buford's Division
N.B. Forrest, Army of Tennessee
Born November 24, 1848, Enlisted November 24, 1863
1938 - 90 years young

Mag Henesy

One of the veterans I met at Gettysburg was an old Negro veteran by the name of Mag Henasy. He lived at 609 Mill Street, Vicksburg, Mississippi, He was a major fifer, and he played a tune for me on the fife. He was born at St. Joseph, Tensaw Parish, Louisiana on June 10, 1844 as a slave. he was captured by Union soldiers at Bruinsburg, Mississippi about 75 miles south of Vicksburg when his "old boss", James M. McGill, "was taking all of us away from the plantation as the Yankees were coming." He was taken to Warrington, Mississippi by the Union soldiers where he volunteered in June 1863.

He drilled with a gun, but never got to shoot it. He was soon given a fife as he was, with his old master a "Quill Blower". Every Sunday, the master had him play a couple of tunes on his Quills. "He was a fine old man," he said, "a Scotsman." Mag Henasy enlisted in the 53rd Colored Regiment. He participated in the siege of Vicksburg. He went to Grand Gulf where they had a battle. Then he went to Fort Gibson on the Mississippi, then to Yazoo City and to Fort Smith, Arkansas where they had a big battle. As a musician, he marched his regiment up to the front of the line, then they would fall back and stack their drums, put their fifes in their haversacks or pockets, and then assist the doctors in administering to the wounded. He was mustered out on March 10, 1866, at Vicksburg, and has been there ever since.

Julius Franklin Howell
Bristol, Virginia

Age 92 - served as a corporal in CO "K", Virginia Cavalry,
    Fitzhough Lee's Division, Ewell's Corps, C.S.A.
Was a history teacher - taught school for 28 years in Arkansas
His "young" wife along
    handed out a paper at Gettysburg

The following was given to me by this veteran in Gettysburg 1938, 75th reunion.

    Comparative Longevity Vitality, and Activity
    Lieut. General Julius Franklin Howell, U.C.V.

Born January 17, 1846

Many times in recent years, I have been asked the secret? of my longevity, the query was intended to include vitality and activity, my reply in substance has been:

1. I started in life with a robust father and a splendid mother, of course, I had no concern with this combination, I simply mention it for its bearing on eugenics, and the importance of physical well-being to posterity.

2. I was brought up on a farm in Eastern Virginia, hence had the benefit of pure rustic air and the plain substantial food common to the country; my father was a minister of the Gospel, and hence wholesome discipline and Christian influence had a proper place in shaping my character.

3. From by early boyhood till after the breaking out of war between the states. I attended with little interruption the best schools then in vogue, spending much time and effort in memorizing Latin "irregulars", chewing upon Greek roots as a condiment I was required to tackle the problem of mathematics: possibly these activities had little direct effect on my longevity, but the training reacted in a beneficial way.

4. I can not see that my experience of three years as a Confederate soldier has had any special influence except possibly through my high appreciation of the many courtesies extended by the United Daughters of the Confederacy, thus causing me to feel that I am living to some purpose, if nothing more than to know that the memory of our efforts is kept green.

5. At the age of twenty-four, I won the hand and heart of the sweetest girl in all the country-side; and all along for sixty-three years we shared our joys and sorrows; we brought up and educated a family of seven; their filial love and loyalty more than compensated for our efforts in their behalf.

6. During my whole life, I have been reasonably emperate; I have been prudent in caring for my health, and

have suffered little illness; even when a soldier I abstained from strong drink, in which many of my comrades and even higher officers sometimes intemperately indulged.

7. I have always tried to be optimistic, avoiding pessimism as a decadent factor in the life of those yielding to its deteriorating influence; I have tried to enjoy the humorous side of life, as tending to brighten the view of surroundings; I have tried to avoid unfair criticism of the weak and unfortunate, and to sympathize with the "forgotten man".

8. I try to avoid the rusting tendency of idleness by keeping employed in some useful occupation, looking forward rather than backward, and having in view the higher aims of life. Feeling the importance of maintaining a sound body as a suitable associate of a sound mind, I have always taken at least a moderate degree of physical exercise; and even now at the age of ninety-two, I take my "daily dozen".

9. During the past four years, I have been blessed with the companionship of a congenial second wife of middle age, who cheerfully ministers to my needs and comforts.

10. Probably the greatest element conducing to my longevity is my supreme appreciation of moral and spiritual values; I am trying to "grow old gracefully"; to "love the true, the beautiful and the good", "to exalt the ideals of Christianity and to love its eternal truths"; my church being representative of these ideals is first with me; it activities in worship, study of the Holy Scriptures, and deeds of beneficence appeal to me as most noble and worthwhile; I have no fear for the future, and am ready when the father calls.

11. Probably there are other elements that enter into the foundation of a long life, but the above practically cover the ground in my own experience.

J. F. Howell
Bristol, Virginia
February 24, 1938

Basil Lemley
Mt. Morris, PA

Born February 10, 1843, at Marietta, Ohio, on a farm.
Mustered into service in June, 1861, at Pittsburgh, PA in the
    8th Pennsylvania Reserves, CO "I" (190th
    Pennsylvania) for three years.
First battle was at Drainesville, VA in 1801, next battle was on
    the Peninsula. He was in the seven days fighting
    including the last one at Malvern Hill. He was within 4
    miles of Richmond - could see the top of the cupola.
Was wounded on May 6, 1864 in the right shoulder - by a rifle
    bullet - on the skirmish line in the Wilderness.
He was a roustabout and wore out 4 regiments. Was at
    Gettysburg, but not engaged. He was left hand man on
    Meade's (sic?) corps at Lee's surrender.
The 13th regiment of Pennsylvania Reserves gotten up by
    Governor Curtin for home defense was the original

Bucktail regiment. Was in service 4 years and 5 days. He was the "best" runner in the Army of the Potomac. President Roosevelt had Mr. Lemley shake hands with a southern veteran at Antietam, September 17, 1937, and the picture was published in all the papers. (The southern veteran was Mr. Miles from Virginia.)

Dr. Oberton H. Mennet
Commander-in-Chief, G.A.R.
1937 - 1938

4903 Rosewood Avenue, Los Angeles, California
Born March 8, 1850, at Vevay, Indiana. Was mustered in
    November or December, 1864 a little past 14.
    Mustered out September, 1865.
Served in 146th Indiana Infantry and was in skirmishes only.
    Was in the reserves at Lee's surrender.

Rosie G. Russell

There was at Gettysburg, an old Negro woman by the name of Rosie G. Russell, nee Glass. Born in 1829, she would have been 110 on December 20, 1938. She was a slave girl who nursed the Union soldiers at Vicksburg. I have her living in Tent 650 (I can't be sure of the number), 6th Street. Her address was 819 West Main Street, Vicksburg, Mississippi. I cannot find her name listed in "The Seventy-Fifth Anniversary of the Battle of Gettysburg - a report of the Pennsylvania Commission", but she was there. I know she was there because I talked to her and took her picture drinking a bottle of soda.

John F. Sims.
Box 553, Kountz, Hardin County, Texas.

Born Lancaster, South Carolina, September 4, 1844.
Mustered into service January 4, 1864 - weighed 96 pounds.
    Can't read or write - "was off fighting the Yanks when he should have been going to school".
At Lee's surrender at Appomattox Court House, Virginia, April 9, 1865.
Dictated by John Sims, CO "G", 13th Georgia Regiment, Gordon's Brigade, Stonewall Jackson's Corps.
Grant says to Lee: "For God's sake, let's quit butchering our men, you've killed 700 of my men this morning, and I don't know how many I have killed of yours. I have 150,000 men around you, and you have only 7,000 men in all. You have nothing to fight me with. So for God's sake, let's not fight anymore."

Lee says: " I will surrender on conditions."
Grant says: "Make your conditions, and I will accept them."
Lee says: " I will surrender to you my gun's ammunition and war material and nothing else.'
Grant says: "I will accept" and whirled his horse and went back to Yankeedom.
By Blanch McCauley
photo with picture of surrender drawn by Mr. Sims

Mr. D. Vance
Little Rock, Arkansas

Past Commander, U.C.V.
Born June 8, 1845 - Age 95
Served in Cavalry Brigade during the war
Served two years of war
Wears duplicate of General Lee's uniform

William H. L. Wells
Plano, Collen County, Texas

Born September 4, 1840, at Bedford County, Virginia.
    Mustered into the Confederate Army early in the spring of 1861, in the 28th Virginia Regiment. A year later, he was transferred into the Artillery. His first general engagement was Bull Run, July 18 and 21st, 1861. Yankees in retreat. Was in Latham's Battery. Longstreet's Corps at Gettysburg. Fired while Picket's men formed in back of him. Then they came through and the artillery stopped firing temporarily. After Picket's men formed in front of them and marched towards the Union line, the Confederate artillery started firing again until the infantry started up the hill on the

other side, then the Confederate artillery stopped firing so as not to kill their own men.

He fought in twenty battles and never got a scratch. General Lee was a great man, but no better than Joseph Johnson. He fought 4 years in the Confederate army. He was home sick when Lee surrendered.

Chief White Cloud

Another veteran I want to mention is because he was very colorful. He is "Chief White Cloud all over the state of Kansas".

He was born at Highland, Kansas, May 1840, and was a "full-blooded Iowa Indian". At the time, he was in school at Highland under "Father Irwin" when he enlisted at 18 at Fort Leavenworth, Kansas in the 14th Cavalry, and served in no other regiment. Father Irwin was a Presbyterian minister. Several of the boys from this school enlisted.

He fought at Parson's Spring, Camden, and got within 40 miles of Red River. He was never wounded, but got his horses shot from under him twice while on picket duty. He fought on the Little Missouri under Colonel Blair and General Steele.

He owns a necklace of "bear claws" inherited from four generations of "White Clouds". This necklace represented the "Bear" clan of Iowa Indians.

His address at the time (July 5, 1938) was "White Cloud", Kansas, or Rulo, Nebraska, "attention Chief White Cloud".

Thomas S. Aderholdt
(No Photograph)

Born at Catawla, North Carolina, August 27, 1846
Mustered into the Confederate Army at Hanover Junction.
First fight was the battle of the Wilderness about two or three months after he enlisted. Fought at Gettysburg in 32nd North Carolina (Co. "F"), Daniel's Brigade. Was in 1st day's fight and part of 2nd. (had not enlisted)
Went home right after the battle and stayed there until the next spring, when his brother who was in the army, was given a furlough for getting Mr. Aderholdt to enlist. Was a ragged - ed private all during the war.
The way he was at Gettysburg was this:
He went to visit the Confederate Army at Hanover Junction to see his father and brother. The Confederate Army started its invasion of Pennsylvania, and he accompanied it. At Battle of Gettysburg, Colonel Brabbell used him as an orderly, but he picked up a musket, and fought, sometimes, beside his brother. His did not cross the river on the Northern invasion. His regiment did not get to Devil's Den or the slopes of Little Round Top.
Present address (1938): Friarspoint, Mississippi (on the river)

John Shearer
(No Photograph)

12th Wisconsin Battery
Born in Glasgow, Scotland, February 4 1847. Mustered in October 20, 1862, as a mule driver. Carried ammunition for 6 months with the army of the frontier. Mustered out on July 25, 1865, after Sherman received Joe Johnston's surrender at Durhaw, North Carolina.

Ira R. Wildman
(No Photograph)

Troop A, 1st Michigan Cavalry
Danbury, Connecticut
Age 88 (last March, 1938)
"Last man living who carried a gun at his age"
Enlisted in 1864
Mustered out in 1867
Served with Custer

Augustus Owen
(No Photograph)

Dover, Delaware
Served in 50th New York Infantry
Enlisted in 1864, Mustered out at the end of the war
Age 95

O. A. Gilliam
(No Photgraph)

Dallas, Texas
Enlisted in 11862, mustered out in 1865
Served under Pickett

Michael Hawk
(No Photograph)

78th Ohio
Served under Sherman
Enlisted June 1864, mustered out at close of war

George W. Shreve
(No Photograph)

Age 94
Santa Cruz, California
Served in Stuart's Horse Artillery
60 years in California

Charles Levi Marston
(No Photograph)

Age 93
Yarmouth, Maine
1st Maine Cavalry
Enlisted in 1863, mustered out in 1865

Chapter III
Diary Kept by William H. H. Ogden, Sr. During the Last Years of His Enlistment, 1862-1864

My maternal great-grandfather served for three years as an enlisted man in the 4th regiment of the Pennsylvania Reserves Corps. During the last year of his enlistment, he kept a diary. While it does not contain anything spectacular, it might be interesting to share some of his experiences. Before doing so, I want to give some background of the Pennsylvania Reserves Corps, and especially of the 4th regiment in which he served.

On April 15th, the day after the fall of Fort Sumter, President Lincoln issued a proclamation calling for 75,000 volunteers to serve a term of 3 months to put down the rebellion. A request was made to the state of Pennsylvania for 14 regiments. Not waiting for the legislature to act, Governor Curtin issued a call for men. The response was overwhelming, so that almost immediately, the 14 regiments were increased to 25, and before the end of the month, they were organized and in the field.

The national government, at that time, would accept only a limited number of troops. Governor Curtin, realizing that the crisis would not easily be resolved, saw the need for additional troops. He called a special session of the legislature, and legislation was passed to organize and arm a division consisting of thirteen infantry, one cavalry and one light artillery regiments. The purpose was to have ready a disciplined and fully equipped body of state troops for any emergency that might arise, including the request for state troops by the U. S. government.

Two days after the passage of the legislation, Governor Curtin issued a proclamation setting the number of companies that would be required from each county in the state. The same proclamation ordered these companies to convene in state

W. H. H. Ogden
in dress uniform

W. H. H. Ogden, Sr.
in uniform of
Quaker City Guards

Mrs. W. H. H. Ogden (Mary)
wife of W. H. H. Ogden

camps established not only in Harrisburg (Camp Curtin) but in Pittsburgh, West Chester, and in Easton. There the recruits were to be organized and receive military instruction until such time as their service be required for the defense of the state.

Previous to this, many public spirited citizens from all parts of the state, believing that the Army of the United States was wholly inadequate for the maintenance of order and for the protection of public and private property, had organized and maintained, at their own expense, military companies to be ready for those emergencies which they believed would soon come. One of the citizens was Robert G March of Philadelphia, who was active in various military organizations in that city. Among these groups was the "Quaker City Guards", the military company to which my great-grandfather belonged. Having volunteered his service to the governor, Robert G. March was commissioned by the governor on April 23rd to recruit a regiment consisting of six militia companies. Among these was the "Quaker City Guards".

Immediately after the passage of the act creating the Reserve Corps, Governor Curtin invited George A. McCall of Chester County to accept the position of Major General as provided in the law. A graduate of West Point, he was a veteran of the Indian Wars in Florida and the war with Mexico.

On May 27th, Major General McCall directed William B. Mann, Esq. of Philadelphia to take the organized companies of Philadelphia, which had been mustered into state service on May 25th, to Camp Washington in Easton, which had been established on the fair grounds of the city. (This date was important because, when it became time to be discharged from the service, the question was what mustered in date to accept - the state or the federal.)

Thirty companies, along with the six companies organized by Col. March, were to rendezvous there for the purpose of forming regiments of the Reserve Corps. The 4th regiment, consisting of five companies from Philadelphia, including the "Quaker City Guards", and one each from Montgomery, Chester, Monroe, Schuylkill, and Lycoming counties, was organized at Easton on June 21, 1861. The "Quaker City Guards" became Company B of that regiment, and Robert M. McClure was elected captain of the regiment.

The Union force, under Irvin McDowell, was defeated at Bull Run, July 21, 1861. This made it necessary to consider the protection of Washington and required a strong force on the north bank of the Potomac above Georgetown. The Reserve regiments were ordered to proceed to Washington as rapidly as possible. The entire Corps, numbering 15,856 officers and men, were mustered into the service of the United States and became a part of the Army of the Potomac. It would be the only state organization in the history of the war that went into the U.S. service as98 a complete division; it lost more men than any other like number serving the three strenuous years beginning with McClellan's first Richmond campaign.

On July 21, 1861, the Reserves were ordered to break camp and proceed to Camp Curtin, Harrisburg. Remaining there only a short time, they were again ordered to break camp and start for Baltimore, arriving the next day, July 22nd. Colonel March, leaving Harrisburg in advance of the others, was to await the arrival of the 1st regiment west of Baltimore. Early on the morning of July 23rd, the whole command, with the exception of the 4th regiment, took their line of march through the city to the Washington Terminal of the B & O Railroad. The 2nd regiment was transported on the B & O to Sandy Hook, arriving on the 28th of July. The 3rd regiment proceeded directly to Washington, where they arrived the evening of July 25th. The 4th regiment remained in camp near Baltimore. On the 20th of August, the Reserves were temporarily organized into Brigades. The 4th became a part of the 1st Brigade.

On August 22, 1861, the 4th regiment broke camp, leaving Camp Carol near Baltimore; they were to journey to their new camp at Tennallytown. In their march through Washington, on the way to Tennallytown which was five miles northwest of Georgetown, they halted in front of the White House at midnight. President Lincoln, rising from his bed, went out to great them. He addressed the 4th Reserves in the following manner, "Sons of Pennsylvania Reserves, I thank God you are here tonight, and I thank the Governor of Pennsylvania that you are here tonight. I thank Governor Curtin for your splendid organization and in being here tonight at this critical time to save the capital of the nation from the enemy". (Pennsylvania Reserves at Antietam, 2nd Brigade, page 53

      This was not the only occasion in which my great-grandfather would meet Mr. Lincoln. After his term of enlistment had expired in June of 1864, he went to work for the Quartermaster Department in Washington. While here, according to my great aunt, he met and shook hands with Mr. Lincoln at a function in Washington. I have a pair of white kid gloves which I am told he wore on the occasion.

      Col. March resigned October 1, and was succeeded by Col. Albert L. Magilton. Eventually the 4th regiment (33rd Pennsylvania) was assigned to the 2nd brigade 1st Corps. The Brigade commander was General George G. Meade. On the 9th of October, the Reserves broke camp and crossed the Potomac River on what was known as the "Chain Bridge" into Virginia where they encamped in line with the Army of the Potomac which was holding the right of the line neat Langley. Here they joined the forward movement of the army towards the plains of Manasses. From there they moved on to Hunter's Mill where they were engaged in the Seven Days Fighting around Richmond from Mechanicsville to Malvern Hill. At Harrison's Landing, they were personally addressed by General

George B. McClellan who congratulated them on their heroic fighting.

Shortly after this, General McCall had to resign because of ill health, and did not live too long after resigning. The Reserves were next placed under the command of General John J. Reynolds. Under his command, they marched to Manasses where they were engaged in the Second Battle of Bull Run, August 29th and 30th.

Here is a clipping from a newspaper printed some years later concerning my great-grandfather and his participation in the Battle of Bull Run. He is mentioned by name, and the article concerns the sale of a farm in New Jersey. It goes on to say:

"....Mr. Ogden, being in poor health, is compelled to dispose of it. The above named person was a member of the noted Pennsylvania Reserves, and served three years in the war of 1861 - 1865. He tells a very interesting story of his experience at the battle of Bull Run, where he was struck in the left breast by a grape shot and knocked unconscious. The brass plate of his equipment and the notebook he carried in his pocket doubtless saved his life."

I was told that, in addition to his notebook, there was a New Testament that he carried, and an indentation in his New Testament (which I still have) was made from that shell. The ill health which the article mentions was an effect of that grape shot from which he suffered the rest of his life.

After the second Battle of Bull Run (or Manasses), they engaged in a back and forth movement to cover the retreat of Pope's Army from Bull Run to the defense of Washington. From here they marched to South Mountain where they were placed under the command of General George G. Meade in the battle of Antietam.

The 4th regiment marched from Keedysville on the Wiliamsport Road on the 16th of September. When near the Williamsport and Sharpsburg turnpike, the enemy was discovered on the left. The Regiment was ordered forward marching in column by division until they arrived at the woods directly in (their) front.

Here is the account as recorded in my great-grandfather's diary.

September 15, 1862

"This morning our division was relieved - on South Mountain by the Division of General Sedgewick who crossed in pursuit of the Rebels who retreated during the night. Large numbers of stragglers were picked up by the pursuing column. We took up our line of march reaching Keedysville about 3:00 P.M. which was made the headquarters of McClellan. After night our Corps (1st) took position on the east bank of Antietam Creek. The enemy's position was west of the creek on a range of hills a mile back and running parallel with Said (?) Creek.

September 16, 1862

"Salvo opened at daybreak this morning with heavy artillery firing on the left. Rebs could be seen in front in line of battle - (we were) ready to receive them, our position being admirable - country ranking with slight woods.

At 3:00 P.M. our Corps under the command of Hooker crossed the Creek on the extreme right taking the enemy somewhat by surprise. We met the Rebel pickets near Smoketown. Our skirmishers were thrown forward and our column advanced in double quick time.--- We drove them back a couple of miles. When coming on the main body fighting ceased for the night as if by mutual consent. The two armies laid within a few feet or each other for the night perfecting arrangement for the coming conflict.

September 17, 1862

At daybreak, the fight began with terrific firing and continued until night. After a half hours sharp fighting, the enemy began to give way, and were followed through a cornfield to the edge of the woods near Dunkard Church, but, being met by superior force, we fell back halfway to our original position. The cornfield was taken and retaken repeatedly. A fresh corps coming up the Rebs were driven to the cover of the woods. We holding possession of the contested (corn) field in which lay thousands of the Rebel dead and wounded and ours intermingled.

General Hooker had been wounded early in the morning. Meade taking command of the Corps. Brigadier General Mansfield was killed.

September 18, 1862

No renewal of the fighting. Day spent in caring for the wounded and burying the killed. Heavy rain in the afternoon.

September 19, 1862

Advanced against the enemy, but, to our surprise, found he had crossed the River with all his effects. Camped on the bank of the River two miles above Shepardstown.

September 20, 1862

Still in camp. A portion of our forces, in attempting to cross at the Shepardstown Ford, was repulsed. The 118 P.V., the corn exchanged, were badly cut losing about four hundred.

September 21, 1862

Still in camp - quite warm - all quiet."

From Antietam, they proceeded to Fredericksburg where the 4th regiment was actively engaged in the battle of Fredericksburg on December 13th, holding the left of the line of battle.

Nothing is written until **January 19, 1863**; then he recorded several days of marching and camping.

"This is the mud march," he writes, *"the weather lowering so that we are almost choked by the smoke."*

Greatly reduced in number, the 3rd and 4th regiments were ordered to Washington on February 8, 1863. While here, a number of new recruits were assigned to the regiment. They spent almost a year in Alexandria on guard duty, guarding prisoners of war and deserters, etc.

Here are a few things mentioned which were of interest to me.

On **August 3rd**, he tells of taking a walk to visit the colored camp, and on arriving, he found that the first district Regiment had just left for North Carolina.

On **August 4th**, he noted that the thermometer had reached 104 degrees.

August 6th was a day of fasting and prayer by a proclamation of the President.

November 3rd, 1863

"I went to Washington on a pass where I got my teeth cleansed and plugged."

Dr. Sigmond at 290 Pennsylvania Avenue was the dentist, and the cost was $25.00. He tells of helping David Green to fix his tent because he was expecting a visit from his wife.

November 27th, 1863 he writes,

".... good news from the Southwest. Bragg routed by General Grant."

These are two interesting recordings about which I would have liked to know more.

*"**December 7th, 1863** - weather very cold. Congress convened today. The President is reported sick with smallpox."*

December 15th, 1863 he mentions a visit *"to camp by the officers of the Russian fleet"*.

Against the wishes and protests of both officers and men, the 3rd and 4th regiments were to remain in Alexandria until January 5, 1864, when they were ordered to West Virginia in pursuit of the enemy, and the destruction of his supplies.

January 5th, 1864, he writes, *"received marching orders at 3:00 P.M."*

The next morning, they marched to Washington, and had breakfast at the "Soldier's Retreat", and then boarded cars.

Traveling all night, they reached Martinsburg, West Virginia, at 7:00 A.M. on January 7th, where they went into camp at "Faulkness Woods". It began snowing in the afternoon, and, having no tents, they took shelter wherever they could. He, with several of his comrades, took shelter in the "Faulkness House".

On January 28th, they left Martinsburg for New Creek, a wild and desolate mountain region 100 miles west of Martinsburg. Early on the night of January 31st, in the midst of a severe rain, sleet, and snowstorm, the regiment started in pursuit of the enemy who had attacked a wagon train of 80 wagons going from New Creek to Parkersburg, West Virginia. It was march and counter march for six days, but the enemy got away.

On February 11th, they marched back to Martinsburg, and on March 27th were ordered to Harper's Ferry where they were to spend a short time protecting the railroad and guarding prisoners.

March 26th, 1864, he records,

"*Received orders to pack for a march.... turned tents into the commissary, loaded knapsacks aboard cars, and marched to Harper's Ferry*" where they "*reported to General Sullivan at the Division Guard House on Hall's Island where prisoners of war, federal prisoners and deserters were confined - took quarters in the Cotton Mill.*"

Hall's Island, he tells us, was where, "*the Hall's Rifle and Carbines were formerly manufactured. The fine buildings were all burned by the Rebel forces after the battle of Antietam and are a pile of ruins.*"

March 29th, 1864, he continues,

"Hall's Island is situated in a narrow valley between Loudon (?) and Bolivar Heights, a half mile above the Ferry. It is formed by an artificial water course cut for mill power."

They were to remain here until April 3rd, when they were ordered back to New Creek. from here they would go to Webster, West Virginia, and then on to Brownstown, 10 miles above Charleston, West Virginia where they would join General Crook's expedition up the Valley of the Kanawha River.

He describes this journey. Traveling over the mountain in a snowstorm, they laid overnight at Grafton. The next morning, about 4 miles from Grafton, they got off the cars, and camped in the wood east of Webster, West Virginia.

April 6th, 1864. he writes,

"The roads are in a horrible condition. Received orders in the afternoon to turn in all surplus baggage...everything packed and ready to move. The wagons, ambulances, and pontoons going on to Parkersburg, but their movement was delayed."

April 7th, they were still in camp, and he has a touch of spring fever.

"All the supplies are being sent to the front. A requisition was sent in for rifles for our regiment."

April 8th, still in camp near Webster, West Virginia, he writes,

"Each man is ordered to have two pairs of shoes, and to pack all supplies, clothing, rations in knapsacks."

The weather was miserable, and the 12th Regiment, Virginia Infantry started for Beverly on April 9th, but had to return because the roads were impassable. The next day, running short of rations and having eaten all of his hard tack, he found a friend in the 3rd Regiment who had a good supply and was kind enough to divide it with him. The rations finally came in, and they *"had a full benefit of a supper on hard tack"*.

"Webster is located on the Branch of the B & O railroad, 4 miles from Grafton and also on Nine Fork, a branch of the Tiger Valley River which runs by Grafton. The country is very hilly, but not mountainous in this section. The houses are all framed or log, mostly one and a half stories high. The only building of likely appearance, with the exception of one dwelling, is a large Grist Mill five stories high. There are about 100 houses in the village. The Depot is little more than a shed."

April 12th, he continues,

"The weather is still miserable, and the roads are in a horrible condition. The 12th Virginia regiment has just come in from Beverly. They say a mule train cannot haul sufficient forage for subsistence to Beverly and return. My private opinion is that the intended expedition will not be prosecuted for some time."

April 14th,

"for a wonder" there was no rain, but *"the sky is still clouded. The paymaster, Major Reynolds - the brother of our*

lamented General - was in camp today making the hearts of many to rejoice, but others, I suppose, feel rather down as they think of their heavy Sutter bills. Troops still continue to go forward. The destination, I suppose, is Clarksburg or Parkersburg."

April 15th, he received pay for the months of January and February, and writes, *"some of the boys are quite lively with the effects of a liquid manufactured from Rye."*

He, along with Sergeant Anderson, left camp at 2:00 P.M. with *"the purpose of hunting some eggs."* They got as far as Prunytown, and *"met William Billings and Marks of I Company, and bought a few necessary articles, and started out the Clarkesburg Pike for the intended purpose of getting some supper, but was unsuccessful."*

They *"called at a house and were cordially impressed by a young lady to come in and take some seats. Went in after conversing for a short time. Two other young ladies came by and were invited to step in after an agreeable conversation. One of the ladies played on the piano and sang the 'Bonnie Blue Flag' with the stripes and stars being an offset to 'The Bonnie Blue Flag with a Single Star', also many other pieces. Spent 2 hours being agreeable and then returned to town and took supper at the Taylor House kept by William G. W. Bogese."*

The Town (Clarkesburg?), I judge, contains about two thousand inhabitants. The principal buildings are three churches, a Court House, and a jail. Returned to camp about 8:00 P.M., and found six days rations being served with orders to march at daybreak. Marching orders postponed because of weather - rain and snow."

April 18th, Webster, W.Va.

"*The weather today has been pleasant. Majors General Ord and Sullivan with their representative staffs rode through the camp this morning. Three hearty cheers were given for General Ord. Turning to General Sullivan, he said, 'These are some of my old boys.' Turning again, he said, 'How are you, boys, glad to see you. I will try to find something for you to do soon.'.*"

Because of the inclement weather, they were to remain in camp in Webster, W.Va. for a little over two weeks.

April 19, he writes that there is a report that General Sigel is to be relieved and General Ord is to take command of the Department. "*Reports say that Sigel is to go to Tennessee*".

April 20th, Webster, W. VA, he continues,
"*...a very disgraceful affair took place in my tent last night. At 9:00 P.M., Sergeant Anderson and myself went to bed. During the night (about 12 o'clock, I judge) I was awakened by disputing and loud talking. I roused up and found that two of the inhabitants with two others were playing cards - a very pernicious game called Bluff. Lieutenant G.C.W. being one of the party, the others being J.G.L., D.G.R., and P.H._ (?). They passed around a canteen, the contents of which I supposed to be fire water. The rowe finally ended in a fight between J.G.H. and P. H._. Will Moorehouse also entered in. Got all the buttons .... torn off his shirt for which he is going to fight, so he says. D.G.R. got a black eye, P.H._ a skinned face. The Lieutenant made his exit. So ended a sociable game of gambling with whiskey drinking.*"

On April 22nd, they were packed and ready to move. A part of the 12th Virginia started at 11:00 P.M. for Parkersburg. All turned in, not expecting to move before morning., but about 11:00 P.M., they received orders to move. Boarding cars, they started about 2:00 A.M., and laid over at Flemington till 5:00 on the morning of the 23rd, and then, they were enroute to Parkersburg. At Parkersburg, he took a walk around the town with Sergeant Anderson.

The next morning along with Sergeant Anderson and William Kramer, they took a walk uptown and got a shave. In the area where the churches were located, they found a loyal church built since the war. It evidently was a Methodist Church since he writes that it was "Quarterly Meeting time". They went in and attended a "Love Feast". While here, they listened to some of *"the experiences of the old pioneers of West Virginia"*, and he writes that they *"greatly benefited"* from this visit.

From Parkersburg, they went on to Wheeling, and, from here, they embarked on a steamer, and journeyed down the Ohio River to Brownsville where they would join General Crook's forces. In boarding the steamer "Lizzie Martin", he writes, ".... *I met with a great mishap. I lost my gun overboard in 25 feet of water. I suppose I will have to pay for it which is $13.35"*.

April 25th, he awoke *"after a good night's sleep, and found the boat just turning into Pomeroy for coal. Pomeroy is on the Ohio shore. From appearances, it is a great coal depot for the Ohio steamers. There are a great many coal pits along the edge of hills which rise abruptly in the rear of the town. The town is small and mostly framed."*

Proceeding down the river, they reached Point Pleasant at the mouth of the Great Kanawha. Going up the Kanawha, they had to take on a pilot.

April 26th,

"On arriving at the shoals near Charlestown, the boat, being too heavily laden, the regiment had to get off and walk above it opposite the town where they took on another pilot. It's becoming dark," he continued, *"I lay down and took a good long nap from which I woke this morning feeling greatly refreshed."*

They found the boat tied to the shore at Camp Pirott. After boarding, the boat pushed to the western shore where they landed and went into camp.

April 27th, General Order No.1 was issued from Headquarters Brigade, 3 Division, Army of West Virginia, from Colonel Sichels, 3rd P.R.V.C. Commanding announcing his staff officers. The 3rd and 4th along with two other regiments had been formed into a brigade under the command of Colonel Sichels. These troops were to move up through the Kanawha Valley to Fayetteville and Raleigh over Great Top Mountain.

April 29th, he and another man got a pass and went to Malden and got their boots mended *"which was opportune as we have orders to march tomorrow at 6:00 A.M."*

Everything which would hinder their march was stripped from them and at Brownsville an extra search was made to make sure that the *"least article one possessed"* had been confiscated.

On **Saturday morning, April 30, 1864**, they began their long march up the narrow Kanawha Valley. There were no bridges or pontoons on which to cross. They had to ford the mountains and streams sometimes waist deep. This expedition was intended to reach the Tennessee and Virginia railroad which was one of the main arteries supplying Lee's army.

Beginning their march at 6:00 A.M. with the 4th Regiment in advance, they took the road up the west bank of the Kanawha. While some parts of the road were in good condition *"there were many bad places where the command would be stretched out to a considerable length. There was not much scenery. The road followed closely the river with high mountains on either side. We had three creeks to wade through, two of which were above our knees in depth"*.

May 2nd, they left camp at $6^{1}/_{2}$ o'clock with four days rations taking the road to Fayettesville. They marched from the Great Falls at the head of the Stanley and New River, which is a tributary to the Kanawha River and crossed Cotton Mountain. When they began their ascent up the mountain, it was a beautiful day. In two hours, they were going through the clouds and when they reached the top, there was a raging rainstorm. My great-grandfather writes, *"traveled over tortuous roads all day... marching through a heavy rain storm which started about 1:30 P.M. and drenched us to the skin."*

While on the mountain, it began to snow, and descending from the mountain into Fayette Valley, they ran into a *"regular blizzard"* so that he writes,

"an overcoat would be very agreeable. I am afraid I shall be compelled to throw mine away. I have too much of a load to carry on a long march. Many have thrown away both their coats and blankets. The report of the government to keep

us till the expiration of our U.S. muster is still creating great discontent."

While crossing the Great Flat Top Mountain, fire was set on each side of the road by order of General Crook so that their progress could be seen by the cavalry. This was a signal not only to their own forces, but to the enemy. When the rebels discovered what was being done, they threw obstacles in their way by cutting trees and leaving them fall across the mountain road. There was no room to turn aside to pass them. They had to be removed. When night came the fire could be seen burning for miles around and *"it was amusing to see the men busy extinguishing the fire on the covers of the ammunition wagons.'*

"I saw General Crooks today for the first time," my great-grandfather wrote, *"he does not look to be over 28. I supposed him to be pretty well advanced in age."*

At the crossing of the Pine Run, they came across extensive fortifications thrown up by the Rebs in 1861.

"If defended by a couple of thousand men, it would be a very difficult matter to cross. I hear there is a Reb camp about 35 miles from here. I suppose we will see some of them tomorrow." He continues, *"May 5th, left Beaver Creek about 5 o'clock. Crossed a flat top mountain. Got to the summit about 12:00 noon. From there to the camp for the night, the road was densely blockaded with felled trees which had to be cleared by the Pioneers. We marched a distance of 21 miles from Beaver Creek reaching campground about dusk. I feel very foot sore and tired."*

The next day, **May 6th**, after marching 17 miles over rough mountain road, they reached Princeton where their advanced forces came upon a number of the enemy building trenches. From there, there was a two day's forced march and skirmishing with several of the enemy along the way.

May 7th, he continues,

> "We took up our line of march early this morning taking the road to Wytheville 53 miles distant. Crossed Rocky Mount, our regiment in advance. Met with sharp skirmishing all the way to Rocky Gap. Our regiment crossed Wolf Mountain by climbing, fetching us $1^{1/}_{2}$ miles in rear of the Gap. Encamped for the night."

May 8, 1864

> "Left camp near Rocky Gap about 5:00 A.M., and took up our line of march. Traveled some 28 miles. Our regiment was the wagon guard. Fired on by bush whackers. Wagon guard did not get into camp till 10:00. Felt very foot sore and tired."

> "Passed through some splendid country. Narrow valleys, but rich and well cultivated. As our forage had all run out, the wagons were filled from the full barns along the road."

After passing through Rocky Gap, the army bivouacked for the night near Cloyd's Mountain.

On the morning of **May 9th**,

> "Left camp at half past two. skirmishing began with the rear guard of the enemy at the base of the mountain. .... The enemy was in a strong position on Cloyd's Mountain."

Colonel Sickel's brigade was posted at the south base of the mountain, and was ordered to direct its charge up the slopes, with the 3rd Regiment in front and on the left of the 4th. The enemy opened with terrific fire that took deadly effect. The troops pressed on until within 200 yards of the entrenchment, and them opened fire. Three color bearers in the 3rd Regiment were shot down. It was quickly discovered that the continuance of such a direct assault would produce unnecessary carnage. It was decided that the 1st Brigade should move rapidly to the left oblique so as to secure more protection by the hill. My great-grandfather wrote,

" The first brigade took a by-road to the left to cross the mountain, and take the enemy's position on the right flank. Companies of the 3rd Brigade were sent across the mount in front to force them back while the main column advanced up the main road."

"The Rebs were driven from their position with the loss of two cannons, several limbers, and caissons. The enemy was driven beyond Dublin Depot when night closed the pursuit. A large amount of commissary goods, ammunition, grain, all the supplies for a large army were left behind. After the fight, our regiment was detailed to care for the wounded and pick up the guns. About dark, we moved on to Dublin with about 100 prisoners."

"One remarkable fact which I noticed was that before the sounds of our victorious guns had ceased to be heard, the colored people began to flock to the folds of the Banner of Freedom"

They lost 107 killed and 500 were wounded and missing. Captain Lenhart, commanding the 3rd Regiment was severely wounded, and Colonel Woolworth of the 4th was killed. He was replaced by Lieutenant Colonel Thomas T.B. Tapper.

Leaving Dublin the following day at 5 o'clock, he continues,

"we supplied ourselves as much as possible from the Reb commissary which consisted of hams, dried beef, bacon, etc. The column took the route down the railroad destroying culverts, telegraphs, woods, water stations, etc. In nearing the large bridge crossing at New River (a large structure used by the Tennessee and Virginia Railroad), the Rebel skirmishers were met and driven across where they had a splendid position covering the Bridge. Our artillery was gotten into position under a heavy fire" - the 4th Regiment supported the battery.

"In about an hour's time, the Rebel Batteries were driven out of position. Shortly, their whole line was in full retreat, and our forces advanced to the river and burned the bridge, water tanks and commissary. In retreating, the enemy burned the extensive machine shop at the Central Depot."

The Confederate report states that in the battle of Cloyd's Mountain, their forces numbered 4,000 under the command of General Jenkins, who was mortally wounded in the engagement. The Union forces were 3,800, not including the cavalry which was not engaged.

The command crossed New River at Pepper's Ferry in a large flat-bottomed boat. The cavalry and ammunition wagons were forced to ford the rapid stream. General Crook was concerned for his ammunition train as a number of cavalry men and horses were drowned in the crossing. *"The column moved on down the river, crossing at the Ferry, and camped on the bank of the river for the night."*

"After striking Dublin Depot (a supply station of the enemy), the country becomes more open and broken opening out into a fine valley well cultivated." In marching to New River, there was another skirmish with the enemy.

May 11th, he goes on, we

"left camp at New River at 7:00 A.M. taking the route to Blacksburg. It appears that our hardships are but commencing. Scarcely had we left camp before rain began to fall in torrents drenching us to the skin. We went into camp at Blacksburg - a hothole of Secesh. The town contains, I should judge, about 1,200 inhabitants. To add to our miseries, the rations have about run out so we shall be compelled to live off the resources of the country. .... The rebel news from the Army of the Potomac is very encouraging. It is reported that Lee has been driven back to Richmond with heavy loss of men and four generals."

*"On **May 12th**, left camp at Blacksburg at 5 o'clock. Reached Newport about 10 o'clock had a light skirmish with the cavalry. Routed them with a few shells. They retreated on the Narrows. Our forces took the road to Lewisburg. We began the ascent of Salt Pond Mountain which is 18 miles across. We encamped on the summit for the night. There is a lake on the top of this mountain which I judge to be 3/4 of a mile in length over against 150 yards in width. It has been a disagreeable day. Rain falling all the time."*

On this march, it was necessary to destroy a portion of their wagon train as the road became so bad and the mountain streams so swollen that the traveling became very difficult.

May 13th he continues, we

> *"left camp on the summit of Salt Pond Mountain at 5 o'clock. Passed a very disagreeable night. Rain falling most of the night."*

After traveling the mountains all day, they camped for the night at the junction of the road to Lewisburg and the Narrows.

> *"The Rebels today,"* he writes, *"showed signs of demoralization. Our advance coming in contact with a party, they abandoned a gun with limber, one caisson, and twelve wagons first having strewn all of their content along the road and in the bush which consisted of ammunition, rations, and medical stores, with camp equipage."*

Continuing he wrote,

> *"Passed a very disagreeable night being on guard duty. Rain falling most of the might till ten this morning. Marched at 12 (May 14th) over one of the most horrible roads I have ever traveled across a mountain for six miles.'*

After camping all night,. they left camp the next morning at 7:00 A.M. *"At Sulphur Spring,"* he continued, *"the country opened out into a beautiful valley. Encamped near Union. Got a little meal today - the first we have had with the exception of meat for three days. I begin to feel very weak and worn out."*

> *"**May 16th** - Left camp at Union at 8 o'clock taking the route to Anderson's Ferry. Had pretty good marching as the country has opened enough for us to march in the fields most of the day. Crossed one very bad mountain where we had

to push up the teams, the horses and mules having become exhausted. Reached camping ground within a half mile of the Ferry."

The next day, raining most of the day, they were troubled by bush whackers, and succeeded in crossing the ferry by 2:00 P.M., and marched to Meadow Buff, foraging all the way. They reached Meadow Buff on the 19th of May after 20 day of continuous marching, half of the time skirmishing with the enemy. Every night during this march, strong guards had to be posted around the camp for fear of surprises. For subsistence the men had to depend upon the countryside, and by the time they had reached Meadow Buff, the men had been suffering for three days without food, and over 200 men were without shoes in a wild mountainous country.

In crossing the mountain before coming to Meadow Buff, my great-grandfather wrote,

"*having fallen to the rear for the purpose of relief, a squad of stragglers were fired upon by bush whackers. No one was injured. I learned from one of the Virginia men who had a sister living at the Springs that there was a squad of eighteen loitering among the mountains, they having fired six shots at her husband the might before.*"

May 20th, while at Meadow Buff, he writes,

"*quite a number of citizens have come in today for the purpose of getting transportation north. After arriving in camp, we had a joyful sight, a supply train had just come in from Gauley. We received coffee, sugar, but no crackers. They will be issued in the morning.*"

"For the information of any of my friends who may in all probability see this, I will make a short but true statement. On the 11th instant, while at Blacksburg, we received two crackers for three men, and a 1/2lb. of bacon per man, and about 3 ounces of meal. Also on the 14th, we received a half-pint of meal per man. This, with a spoonful of coffee issued on the 13th, was all we received from the commissary. With the exception of a little wheat on the 10th, the remainder we got by foraging for three days. We were in a mountain district where we could get nothing but fresh meat, and, a part of the time, we had no salt so one can judge the consequences."

After camping at Meadow Buff (42 miles from Gauley), they unexpectedly received order to march at 10 o'clock on May 22nd. They marched about 10 miles to Millville which *"consisted of a small Grist Mill, about 3 houses and a blacksmith shop. I should remark that only our Brigade marched this morning. The remainder of the Division was still at the Buffs."*

While at Millville, he writes on the **23rd**,

"Anderson (Sergeant) succeeded after much trouble in getting a little soft soap for the purpose of trying to get some of the dust out of our clothing which had become quite filthy by our long marches without the opportunity of washing."

"We had glorious news tonight while on dress parade which concerns us all - it was an order from the War Department ordering that the 3rd and 4th Reserves should be discharged from the date of the muster-in of the companies which is the 25th instant for us. If spared, I hope to be home by the 25th of next month."

May 27th, he mentions that they are still in camp at Millville, and the *"the men are beginning to show impatience at the delay in getting mustered out as they had understood was the intention."*

And on **May 28th**, he writes, *"Great indignation is expressed by the men on account of the delay caused in getting to the rear, and of a report that the regiment will have to go on a ..... raid to Stanton."*

When the army in the Shenandoah Valley was driven back from Stanton, there was talk of sending General Crook's army in Western Virginia as reinforcements. Obviously this did not happen.

Still remaining in camp, he attended divine services held by Chaplain Horne of the 4th in the morning and Chaplain Pomeroy of the 3rd in the afternoon, and he writes, *"had a very good attendance and a very attentive audience. Their term of service of three other companies expired today making five (companies) in all that have expired. The men have refused all further duty. The discontent is still increasing. A report now exists that General Crook intends keeping us till the 20th day of June. Dress parade ordered for six o'clock. The men refuse to go out."*

"Good news today", he writes on **May 30th**, *"all men whose time expired before the first of July are to return with the regiment to the state. All those whose term expires after that date together with other veterans were transferred to other commands which were to remain with the division."*

Returning to Meadow Buff, they went into camp for the night. There they drew 3/4 rations for two days, and continued to General Crook's headquarters, where their teams were exchanged. They had to *"take more worn out animals leaving the fresher ones"*. After breaking camp, they moved on towards Lewisburg where they had a *"pretty rough march --- crossing two mountains, Big and Little Sewell --- the former nine miles across."* They marched 22 miles, and he writes, *"Feel very tired, sore and weak. The weather clear and warm."*

    Leaving camp on **June 1st**, they left camp at 4:30 A.M., and marched 25 miles reaching Gauley about 3:00 P.M. where they crossed the river and camped for the night about a mile below the ferry.

    "The men are pretty worn out. I believe I never felt so nearly exhausted since being in the army as I do at the present time. If it was not for good prospects ahead I could not stand the marching. The weather is hot and sultry."

    On June 3rd, they began marching at 4:30 A.M. reaching Camp Pirott at 3 o'clock, stopping for two hours at noon and ten minutes every hour for a distance of 22 miles. Their expected boat (the Jonas Powell) arrived on June 4th, and they boarded at 9:00 A.M. and started down the river, reaching Gallipolis at 5:00 P.M. where they took on coal and got some rations. At Parkersburg, they halted at 10:00 A.M. for a half hour where he went ashore and purchased some bread. Continuing up the river stopping at a couple of places, they reached Beaver (a small town on the Ohio) about dusk where the boat *"ran hard and fast on the shoals"*. Here they were compelled to get a lighter (flat bottom boat used for loading and unloading ships that are not brought into a wharf or harbor) and go ashore at Phillipsburg where the boys, he wrote, *"scared the good people of the town by hallooing so they went into their houses closing their doors and window* blinds. *About ten o'clock, the boat was gotten off and we all got aboard, leaving the good people to get over their fright."*

On the 7th, they reached the shoals at what he called the *"glass house at 9 o'clock, which is five miles below Pittsburgh"* where they went ashore and marched to Pittsburgh through Allegheny City. Here they got "dinner at the Volunteer Refreshment Saloon over the Market House". They then boarded cars at 5:00 P.M. for home via Harrisburg. Traveling all night they reached Harrisburg about noon the next day (the 8th). Proceeding on, they reached Philadelphia about 7:00 P.M. He writes,

"being almost entirely unexpected nevertheless, we had a large escort down Market to 20th, down 20th to Chestnut, up Chestnut to 3rd, up 3rd to Mechanic's Hall where speeches were made and a bountiful collation (a spread of food) prepared which was partaken of by all those who wished. I went to my sister's house, 612 Sylvester Street, where I found them anxiously awaiting my arrival. In the meantime Thomas was on the search for me, also Brother Jos."

On the 9th, not feeling well, he did not report to the Regiment, but later he made a Street Parade, and *"took dinner at the Refreshment Saloon of the Cooper Shop"*, and went to visit his sister Rachel in the afternoon.

June 20th, he writes,

"after some delay, we finally succeeded in getting mustered out and paid today in full."

This ended his term of service after three years in the Army.

SURVIVORS OF ANTIETAM UNVEIL FOUR MONUMENTS

Pennsylvania's Grizzled Veterans Gather Around Field Where Comrades Fell Fighting for "Their Altars and Their Firesides."

PENNYPACKER REVIEWS ORGANIZATION OF RESERVES

Third, Fourth, Seventh and Eighth Regiments and Their Valorous Deeds Now Commemorated in Enduring Granite and Symbols of Victory.

Special Despatch to "The Press."

Hagerstown, Md., Sept. 17.—Civil War veterans from Pennsylvania held full sway on Antietam battlefield to-day, the forty-fourth anniversary of the bloody conflict. The four pretty monuments erected to the memory of the members of the Third, Fourth, Seventh and Eighth Regiments of the Pennsylvania Reserve Corps who fell at Antietam were unveiled and formally dedicated by the survivors of the respective organizations.

This afternoon the monuments were transferred by the commission to the State of Pennsylvania and in turn to the United States Government, these exercises being held in Antietam National Cemetery, at Sharpsburg. Governor Samuel W. Pennypacker, accompanied by members of his staff, attended the exercises and occupied seats upon the rostrum with the other speakers.

Monument of the 128th Regiment, Pennsylvania Volunteers, which was dedicated on the Antietam battlefield yesterday.

Former Chaplain Prays.

Alexander F. Nicholas, of Philadelphia secretary of the Antietam Battlefield Commission, presided at the exercises which opened with prayer by Rev. Dr Judson Furman, of Pittsburg, formerly chaplain of the Seventh Pennsylvania Reserves. General John A. Wiley, of Pittsburg, treasurer of the Monument Commission, transferred the monuments to the State of Pennsylvania and they were accepted by Governor Pennypacker who in a brief speech said:—

Upon occasions like this, the anniversary of a great struggle enacted here upon this bloody field forty-four years ago, we naturally become reminiscent. A company of soldiers raised during the early part of the war in the village in which I was born afterward became a company the Pennsylvania Reserves." A woman, now the leading "lady" of the great Commonwealth of Pennsylvania," then a young girl, with other girls, helped to sew together the uniforms that these soldiers wore. I saw the "Reserve" in the caps they" wore before they departed, and I saw them when they came back from service.' Now, the last ceremony in which I am called by the State of Pennsylvania to participate, is the dedication of these four monuments erected to the memory of the members of the Pennsylvania Reserves who fell at Antietam.

It is with a feeling of satisfaction that I see gathered here so many survivors of that brave corps of men. But one State in the Union had an entire division in the Federal Army during the Civil War. That State was Pennsylvania, and that division was the Pennsylvania Reserves. It was the Pennsylvania Reserves who gained the first victory for the Army of the Potomac at Gainesville.

Raised 17,000 Recruits.

When Lincoln sat at the Capitol awaiting the approach of the successful Confederate army, when the Confederacy was being recognized by nations abroad and the city of Washington was threatened. It was then that the State of Pennsylvania raised 17,000 recruits in two days, and these men composed the "Pennsylvania' Reserves. Times' have changed and we have changed with them. This is a time of peace and plenty. Ivy such as is about these pillars covers the grave of many a brave soldier asleep in this beautiful cemetery. The timid rabbit crouches in safety beneath the rostrum at our feet. Gathered about me I see men from the North and men from the South, here alike in motive and patriotism, to do honor to those men who fought here forty-four years ago.

The monuments were then in turn presented to the United States Government, the acceptance being by John C. Scofield, chief clerk of the War Department, Washington, who represented the President. Mayor G. L. Eberhart, of New Brighton, delivered the oration, his theme being 'Pennsylvania at Antietam.

The exercises concluded with the benediction by Dr. Furman. The addresses were interspersed with music by the Keedysville Cornet Band.

Woman Did Unveiling.

This morning, at the dedication of the 3d Reserve monument, short addresses were delivered by George Burke, of McKeesburg, and B. Frank Fisher, of Philadelphia. Miss J. P Dauth, of Reading, unveiled the monument

Frederick Markoe, of Philadelphia, spoke at the dedication of the fourth. Addresses also were made by W. F. Vanscoten, of Montrose, and Secretary Nicholas, of the commission. Prayer was offered by Rev. W. H. Ogden, of Philadelphia. Miss Alexine Nicholas, daughter of Mr. Nicholas, unveiled the monument.

John Faller, of Carlisle, and Captain Clark, of Harrisburg, delivered addresses at the dedication of the seventh monument. Rev. Dr. Furman offered prayer. Miss Emma P. Faller, daughter of one of the speakers, unveiled the shaft.

General John A. Wiley, of Pittsburg, delivered the address at the dedication of the eighth monument, which was unveiled by Miss. Mayette McWilliams, daughter of Daniel McWilliams, of Pittsburg. Thomas Hill, of Waynesburg, Pa., delivered a short address and read a poem, after which the exercises concluded with prayer by Lieutenant W. J. Kieston, of Pittsburg.

Pennypacker's Staff There.

Governor Pennypacker was accompanied by Adjutant General Thomas J. Stewart, Brigadier General C. Bow Dougherty, Colonels Frank G. Sweeney, H. L. Holdeman, E. R. Chambers, William F. Richardson, Walter T. Bradley, Albert J. Logan, James M. Reed, Lewis T. Brown, W. G. Price, Jr., L. A. Watres, George Brook, Jr., James Archbald, Jr., Thomas S. Martin, Lewis E. Beltler, Major J. Campbell Gilmore and Captain John C. Delaney.

The 128th Pennsylvania monument, which was not completed when the other twelve Pennsylvania monuments were unveiled two years ago, was dedicated formally to-day. It is located on Cornfield Avenue. Colonel W. S. Haas presided, and there were addresses by Governor Pennypacker, Colonel O. C. Bosbyshell, a member of the commission erecting the monuments, and Mahlon H. Berry, a survivor of the 128th. Miss Bertie Amelia Lingle, of Reading, Pa., unveiled the monument.

About fifty survivors of the 130th Pennsylvania held a reunion to-day at their monument in Bloody Lane. Two hundred and fifty survivors of the famous Philadelphia Brigade spent several hours in their park at Antietam.

The four statues, which were erected by the State of Pennsylvania at a cost of about $2500 each, are located on Mansfield Avenue, at points where the respective regiments formed before going into battle. Each monument is about seventeen feet high. It consists of a massive granite base, upon which there is a life-size soldier of '61. Each of the four figures is in a different attitude. The monuments are but a short distance from the large monument erected to the memory of General Mansfield, who was killed at Antietam, by the State of Connecticut, and within sight of the famous "cornfield."

W. H. H. Ogden, Jr. and daughter
in front of the 4th Pennsylvania Reserve Monument
September 17, 1906

R. O. Partington, grandson of W. H. H. Odgen, Jr.,
and daughter in front of the
4th Pennsylvania Reserve Monument,
93 years later.

Pennsylvania Day
Antietam, Maryland

MONDAY
SEPTEMBER
SEVENTEENTH
1 9 0 6

Antietam Battlefield Commission
of Pennsylvania

John A. Wiley, *Treasurer* Alexander F. Nicholas, *Secretary*

ORDER OF EXERCISES

✠

DEDICATION OF THE MONUMENTS OF THE

3d Pennsylvania Reserve Volunteer Corps
4th Pennsylvania Reserve Volunteer Corps
7th Pennsylvania Reserve Volunteer Corps
8th Pennsylvania Reserve Volunteer Corps

by the Regimental Associations, in the morning between the hours of 9 and 12 o'clock

Transfer of the Monuments to the United States Government

In the National Cemetery, Sharpsburg, at 2 o'clock, P. M

Alexander F. Nicholas, 4th Penna. Reserves
Secretary of Commission, *Presiding*

MUSIC—The American Overture . . . E. Catlin
  Keedysville Band

PRAYER—Rev. A. Judson Furman, D. D.
  Late Chaplain 8th Pennsylvania Reserves

MUSIC—Star Spangled Banner
  Keedysville Band

Transfer of the Monuments to the Governor of Pennsylvania
  Genl. John A. Wiley, Treasurer of the Commission

Acceptance of Same and Transfer to the Government of the United States
  Hon. Samuel W. Pennypacker, Governor of Pennsylvania

Receipt on Behalf of the President of the United States
  Hon. John C. Scofield, Chief Clerk of the War Dept.

MUSIC—Grand Selection of War Songs . Ed. Beyer
  Keedysville Band

ADDRESS
"PENNSYLVANIA AT ANTIETAM"
Major G. L. Eberhart, Late 8th Pennsylvania Reserve Volunteer Corps

MUSIC—America
  Audience led by the Keedysville Band

BENEDICTION—Rev. A. J. Furman
  Late Chaplain 8th Pennsylvania Reserve Volunteer Corps

Informal Reception by the Governor of Pennsylvania and Other Distinguished Guests

Two postcards sent to his family by W. H. H. Ogden from the dedication.

Sharpsburg, Sept. 17, 1906
All well. Have better quarters than I had 44 years ago.
Father

Sharpsburg, Md. Sept. 17, 06
This is where we went to church yesterday morning.
Father

The Dunkard Church
Antietam

ABOUT THE AUTHOR

RICHARD O. PARTINGTON is a retired Episcopal clergyman who has long been interested in the Civil War.

Born and raised in Philadelphia, Reverend Partington was a member of the Sons of Veterans Reserves in his youth, and is currently a member of the Sons of Union Veterans of the Civil War to which he has belonged for sixty-five years. He is a past Commander of the Department of Pennsylvania and a past Commander-in-Chief of the national organization as well as a former chaplain of both groups.

Reverend Partington has been a member of the Union League in Philadelphia for over fifty years where he belongs to their Civil War Round Table. He has also belonged to several other historical organizations and was active in the Masonic organization.

www.ingramcontent.com/pod-product-compliance
Lightning Source LLC
Chambersburg PA
CBHW071452150426
43191CB00008B/1327